Under Attack: Fighting Back

Under Attack: Fighting Back

Women and Welfare in the United States

Mimi Abramovitz

Monthly Review Press • New York

Copyright © 2000 Mimi Abramovitz
All rights reserved.
Library of Congress Cataloging-in-Publication Data

Abramovitz, Mimi
     Under Attack, Fighting Back: Women and Welfare in the
United States / Mimi Abramovitz.— [Updated ed.]
          p. cm.
     Includes index.
     ISBN 1-58367-008-4 (pbk.)
     1. Poor women—United States—Social conditions. 2. Single
mothers—United States—Social conditions. 3. Welfare recipients—
United States—History—20th century. 4. Public welfare—United
States—History—20th century. I. Title.

HV699 .A426 2000
362.83'086'9420973—dc21   99-087575

Monthly Review Press
122 West 27th Street
New York, NY 10001

Printed in Canada
10 9 8 7 6 5 4 3 2

CONTENTS

ACKNOWLEDGMENTS

THIS BOOK REFLECTS MY EXPERIENCES AS A WELFARE worker, college teacher, researcher, and social activist, and my participation in the antiwar, civil rights, and women's movements. But most of all, I have been influenced by the welfare rights movement which I was fortunate to work with in the 1960s and again today. I titled this book *Under Attack, Fighting Back* after a national conference in Oakland, California that I attended in 1992 which was organized by women on welfare. It is to past, current, and future welfare mothers that this book is dedicated.

The process of creating a book depends on the support of others. I am indebted to the many feminist scholars who share my interest in women and the welfare state and who have persistently pursued this research. Martha Davis, Linda Gordon, Roberta Spalter-Roth, Rickie Solinger and Guida West provided useful comments on an early draft of the first edition, although they bear no responsibility for my opinions or errors. Books like this could not be written without the work of the Welfare Law Center, the Center for Law and Social Welfare Policy, the Center on Budget and Policy Priorities, and other advocacy groups who tracked legislative developments that many of us outside the nation's capital could not follow on our own. For this second edition, I would like to thank the many researchers and monitoring projects that document what happened to the women who left welfare since the "reform."

I am also grateful to The Hunter College Center for the Study of Family Policy for its commitment to low-income women. The leadership provided by its director, Jan Poppendeick, herself a scholar and activist; the Center's support for the Welfare Rights Initiative which, led by Melinda Lackey, trains college students and organizers; and the uplift I experienced from my work with the students themselves, made an enormous difference to me as I struggled with the first and second editions of this book. I also drew sustenance from working with the Welfare Reform Task Force of the New York City chapter of the National Association of Social Workers; the Bertha Capen Reynolds Society, the national organization of progressive social workers; the New York City Welfare Reform Network; the Committee of 100 Women, and Community Voices Heard. The hard work of these people and groups along with many others around the nation belies the idea that advocacy is dead.

The first edition of this book benefitted enormously from the skillful editing by Susan Lowes, then the Director of the Monthly Review Press, and Akiko Ichikawa, her assistant who also put in endless hours. The attentive editing of the revised chapters for the second edition by Danielle McClellan, Managing Editor at Monthly Review, ensured continuity and readability. My family and friends provided extraordinary support as I immersed myself in my cluttered study for each edition of this book. May Gruber, my step-mother, applied her keen writing skills to early drafts of the second edition. My husband, Bob Abramovitz, trusted my ideas, read and reread chapters, reminded me to include lead sentences, and offered important intellectual insights and correctives. Perhaps most important, he made sure that I relaxed, went to the movies, hiked in the woods and ate good food. And, he was there—always—when I needed him.

PREFACE

WELFARE HAS BEEN "REFORMED!" THE FIRST EDITION OF this book went to press just prior to the passage of the 1996 federal welfare reform law that dramatically changed the face of the United States welfare state. Although Congress had not yet finalized legislation, it was clear then that the nations's leaders had all but decided to abandon their commitment to the poor by downgrading welfare from a federal entitlement program to a state-operated block grant. And indeed, they did. Most states signed on to the Personal Responsibility and Work Opportunity Reconciliation Act (PRA) in 1997. With this came significant changes—a lifetime limit of no more then five years on welfare benefits, stiffened work requirements, and penalties for single mothers. Most states activated the Personal Responsibility and Work Opportunity Reconciliation Act (PRA) in 1997. The subsequent rapid decline in welfare rolls and costs has led politicians and policy makers to celebrate the success of welfare reform.

But, perhaps they celebrate too soon. It is true, as the media reports, that the welfare rolls have dwindled to all-time lows and that many women have found work. However, early research findings and the experiences of women no longer on welfare present another side of the story. From them we hear that large numbers of former welfare recipients cannot make ends meet or find dependable means of support. In some states the welfare rolls have already begun to rise again.

These immediate results only foreshadow the future of welfare reform. The recent increase in extreme childhood poverty may be another sign of what is to come. Common sense tells us that future economic downturns could eliminate jobs now filled by former welfare recipients; that families will eventually run out of resources that enabled them to take in women and children driven from the rolls; that children will suffer from the chronic lack of child care and health services; and that single mothers become anxious or depressed when they cannot provide the care and emotional support their children need. In brief, the hardships of poverty promise to take their well-known toll on the poor and on the rest of society.

As an entitlement, welfare was guaranteed funding by the federal government. As a block grant, its funding requires regular congressional re-approval. The initial appropriation for the PRA expires in 2002, at which time the entire program must be renegotiated. Welfare's foes have already begun to use reports of the success of welfare reform to push for less spending and harsher measures. Some elected officials want the states to return unspent welfare funds to the federal coffers instead of using them for needed services.

The expiration of the PRA creates an opportunity to undo the harms wrought by those seeking to win elections by bashing the poor, privatizing Social Security, spending budget surpluses on tax cuts for the rich, and otherwise dismantling the wider welfare state. Welfare mothers and advocates can publicize the real impact of welfare reform on the lives of the poor and working poor, promote changes that go beyond damage control to undercutting poverty, and mobilize the growing number of welfare rights and advocacy groups around the country. The opponents of welfare reform make outrageous proposals that continue to pull the debate toward the Right. When advocates of the needy respond with real facts and create their own "outrageous" proposals, success often follows. Advocates have won retractions of harmful state welfare provisions and local living wage campaigns.

I hope that this second edition of *Under Attack, Fighting Back* will contribute to these efforts by detailing what is currently known about the troublesome outcomes of welfare reform, by providing updated information on the welfare rights organizing, and by offering an alternative perspective on the contemporary debates about welfare that continue to take place in legislatures, in the academy, and in the streets. I also hope that it will bring more attention to welfare as a women's issue, a focus which continues to get short shrift in all quarters.

Part 1 of this book, rewritten for this revised edition, examines the recent attack on welfare and the impact that the welfare reforms are having on the work and family life of single mothers and on the wider welfare state. Part 2 looks back into the history of attacks on welfare and single mothers. Like the current assault, earlier assaults also targeted the work and family decision of single mothers. Together, the book's first two parts suggest that in their repeated efforts to retrench public assistance, the nation's leaders have been responding to the fears of employers (that welfare undercuts wages) and to the fears of family-values advocates (that assistance to single mothers seriously challenges the patriarchal status quo). The history shows that poor women and public assistance have been scapegoated regularly to enforce both the work and family ethic; to ease public concerns about other social, economic, and political issues; and to divert public attention from the true causes of the nation's woes.

Part 3 moves us from the legislature into the academy, where explanations of social phenomena are developed in the first place. Despite the fact that public assistance and many other social welfare programs aid individuals through their families, the early literature on the welfare state only rarely included women. For at least the past fifteen years, women in the academy have worked to change this. Women, after all, represent 50 percent of the population and the majority of welfare clients and workers. And the functioning of the family and the wider social order, depends heavily on women's work in the home—work that is underwritten by the welfare state. The academy rarely welcomed and only reluctantly acknowledged this feminist scholarship. Nonetheless, the women scholars fought back, and by bringing women into view, transformed our knowledge of the welfare state.

Part 4, updated to include the expansion of welfare rights activism since the mid-1990s, takes us into "the streets" where the power of capital and the state has been contested throughout the twentieth century and where, contrary to popular wisdom, women have always been active. From the black and white middle-class reformers at the turn of the century to the militant housewives during the Depression to the welfare mothers today, women have provided much of the leadership and the legwork. First they insisted that merchants and landlords keep food, clothing, and shelter affordable so that women can carry out their caretaking work in the home. Then women turned their demands to the welfare state as it gradually began to cover some of these basic needs. When social programs came under attack, women mobilized again to defend them from the budget ax.

Social programs have always been a double-edged sword for women, regulating their lives on the one hand and providing needed resources on the other. The welfare state has always been an arena of political struggle. My wish in detailing this history of women's activism is fourfold: to give visibility to the long neglected efforts of women to produce a better life for themselves and their families; to further the work of welfare rights activists by touching base with the accomplishments of their foremothers, to show that all women benefit from and thus have a stake in social programs, and finally to stress the importance to social change of political pressure from below. As long as we can defy the conflicts of gender, race, and class that have kept us apart, I believe that we can— and must—resist the attack on the welfare state and continue to fight for a society based on equality and justice for all.

PART ONE

Still Under Attack: Women and Welfare Reform

It's time to honor and reward people who work hard and play by the rules. That means ending welfare as we know it—not by punishing the poor or preaching to them, but by empowering Americans to take care of their children and improve their lives. No one who works full-time and has children at home should be poor anymore. No one who can work should be able stay on welfare forever.

—Bill Clinton, 1992[1]

[The Personal Responsibility and Work Opportunity Reconciliation Act] begins with a hymn to marriage and is based on the theory that poverty and social dysfunction are caused by the untrammeled sexuality of poor women.

—Katha Pollitt, 1998[2]

When the system ends for me, it ends for you.

—a welfare recipient, 1999[3]

WELFARE REFORM BECAME A HOT POLITICAL ISSUE IN THE early 1990s. During the 1992 presidential election campaign, Bill Clinton drew frequent and loud applause when he declared that welfare should provide "a second chance, not a way of life." By late 1994, the President's plan to cut welfare had lost ground to the Republicans' Contract With America, which called for ending welfare altogether. In August 1996, Congress passed the Personal Responsibility and Work Opportunity Reconciliation Act of 1996 (PRA), better known as "welfare reform." This historic act, which slashed a wide range of safety-net programs for the poor, ended forty years of direct federal intervention in the nation's social-welfare system and paved the way for an attack on the entire welfare state. For the first time, welfare assistance became a short-term benefit, run by the states, without the guarantee of federal funding.

The long debate over welfare took place in the legislature, on university campuses, and in the streets. In the pages that follow, we will examine the issues from several vantage points. Part 1 will look at the forces leading to welfare reform during the 1980s and 1990s and the impact of these reforms on women and children and on social welfare policy. Part 2 will review the history of welfare as a program just for single parents, a history that makes it clear that the 1990s "reforms" represented only the latest in a long line of assaults on poor women and the programs that serve them. Part 3 will move into the academy, where over the past two decades feminist scholars have struggled to "reform" the standard literature of the welfare state by bringing the lives of real women into view. Finally, Part 4 will take us from the academy into the streets where, contrary to popular wisdom, poor and middle-class women have been fighting for better social programs since the turn of the century.

THE WIDER CONTEXT OF THE ATTACK ON WELFARE

THE TERM WELFARE REFERS BOTH TO SOCIAL PROGRAMS and to the promise of well-being. The discrepancy between this promise of well-being and the actual quality of life for many people has led most western industrial nations, at some point in time, to create a welfare state. Since welfare states determine who benefits from and who pays for government programs, they remain highly controversial. To better understand what happened to the U.S. welfare program for single mothers, we first need to discuss three background issues: the core social welfare programs, the forces behind the latest attack on the welfare, and the ideological underpinnings of the campaign to reform the program.

WHAT IS WELFARE? THE CORE PROGRAMS

THE UNITED STATES LAUNCHED ITS MODERN WELFARE state during the Great Depression of the 1930s, when the collapse of the economy created massive unemployment, major business failures, and mounting social protests. The turmoil, which shook the moorings of the capitalist system, forced Congress to provide emergency relief to all sectors of the economy. The initial emergency programs put cash into the empty pockets of the working poor, and gave banks, farms, and small firms a boost. This temporary government assistance protected thousands of individuals, families, and business establishments from the most devastating effects of the Depression. It also helped to restore the public's faith in the economic and political system and to defuse some of the growing social unrest.

The Depression was supposed to end quickly, the relief programs were supposed to be temporary, and private charities were expected to meet the remaining demand for aid. Instead, the length and severity of the economic crisis forced Congress to acknowledge what it had preferred for so long to ignore: that market economies rarely provide enough jobs or income for everyone and that to prevent chaos and disaffection, the federal government must assume major responsibility for social welfare. After considerable partisan debate, in 1935 Congress reluctantly passed the Social Security Act. This landmark legislation transferred responsibility for social welfare from the states to the federal government, replacing temporary and sporadic state-administered programs with a permanent social welfare system—some thirty to fifty years after most other western industrial nations had taken this step.

15

The Social Security Act established two types of cash benefits: social insurance and public assistance. The social insurance programs included a pension for retired workers (what we informally call Social Security) and Unemployment Insurance, which replaces the wages of those who face temporary unemployment. Social Security is funded by a payroll tax that is paid half by the worker and half by the employer, while Unemployment Insurance is financed through a tax on the employer alone. These programs, which now cover more than 95 percent of all wage earners, have become so well accepted that most people think of them as rights, not as assistance.

The Social Security Act also included three public assistance programs for the poor: Aid to Dependent Children (ADC), Old Age Assistance (OAA), and Aid to the Blind (AB); Aid to the Permanently and Totally Disabled (APTD) was added in 1956. Welfare is the popular name for ADC, which provides financial assistance to children who are continuously deprived of support due to the death, absence, or incapacity of a parent or caretaker. (ADC became known as AFDC in 1962, when Congress passed a limited program for households with an unemployed father.) In 1965, Medicaid and Medicare were added to the Social Security program, and in 1974 OAA, AB, and APTD were combined into a federalized income-support program called Supplemental Security Income (SSI). It was hoped that this consolidation would standardize these programs and reduce their stigma. The only program to be left out of this important consolidation was AFDC, the program which addressed the needs of poor women and children. In 1996, Congress replaced AFDC with Temporary Aid to Needy Families (TANF), Title I of the PRA, popularly known as welfare reform.

In contrast to the positive notion of rights attached to social insurance, Americans think of the public assistance programs in negative terms such as charity, handouts, or the dole. Until the late 1990s, politicians dared not tamper with the social insurance programs for fear of losing too many votes. But as Part 2 shows, no such fears prevented them from repeatedly attacking the welfare program for single mothers.

REASONS FOR THE LATEST ASSAULT ON WELFARE

THE DRIVE TO REFORM WELFARE THAT BEGAN IN THE early 1980s and culminated with the PRA in 1996 was never about welfare alone. In fact, the attack on welfare helped to fulfill other political agendas. Liberal politicians bashed welfare and the poor to establish their conservative credentials. Business and industry turned against welfare arguing that it undercut their profits. The social conservatives used welfare reform to promote their own version of family values that ruled out all but the two-parent, heterosexual household. Other critics believed the attack on welfare for single mothers would weaken the long-standing taboo against cutting or privatizing the more popular entitlements such as Medicare and Social Security.

CHANGES IN THE POLITICAL ECONOMY

THE WELFARE STATE EXPANDED RAPIDLY DURING THE 1940s and 1950s, as Congress improved the Social Security Act programs and introduced new public housing, mental health, and other services. In the 1960s, the War on Poverty added Medicare, Medicaid, Food Stamps, and a host of legal, employment, social service, and anti discrimination laws to the core income-maintenance programs. However, the expansion began to slow in the mid-1970s, once international competition, cheap foreign labor, and the loss of U.S. dominance in the world economy cut into the profits of U.S. corporations. Business executives, who had once counted on social programs to create purchasing power, maintain a healthy and educated workforce, and co-opt social movements, now declared that these same programs no longer met their goals—especially since the export of jobs and production abroad had diminished their stake in the well-being of U.S. workers. The economic security provided by social welfare programs had also strengthened the bargaining power of workers in the workplace, increased the leverage of women vis-à-vis men, and bolstered the overall political influence of social movements. None of this appealed to business leaders, who began to call for less government spending, arguing that it had raised the cost of borrowing money, increased the price of labor, deepened the deficit, and otherwise interfered with profits.[4] The increasingly influential social conservatives argued that welfare undercut family values and personal responsibility, and should therefore be abolished.

Shrinking social welfare became a key feature of government plans to get the economy back on track. The campaign, begun quietly by President Carter in the late 1970s, went into full swing in the early 1980s with the economic recovery plan launched by President Reagan and continued by Presidents Bush and Clinton. The wider strategy sought to promote economic recovery by redistributing income upward, limiting the role of the federal government, cheapening the cost of labor, shrinking social programs, and weakening the political influence of popular movements that might object to these changes.

Implemented in stages during the 1980s and 1990s, welfare reform brought about dramatic changes which were neither accidental nor simply cold-hearted. In fact, the main provisions of welfare reform—cutting the cost and size of welfare, enforcing the work ethic, upholding the family ethic, and ending entitlements—came straight from the pages of the economic recovery plan variously called Reaganomics, trickle-down economics, or deficit reduction.

THE IDEOLOGICAL ARGUMENTS

THE AMERICAN PUBLIC NEVER LOVED SOCIAL WELFARE programs, but it did not necessarily want them dismantled. In fact, by the early 1990s, nearly 50 percent of all households drew on government benefits—from Food Stamps to Social Security to mortgage-interest tax deductions.[5] To win support for a plan that was based on tax cuts for the rich and spending cuts for the poor and middle class, the budget cutters had to create enthusiasm for their plan among those who traditionally supported welfare and among the legions of people who stood to lose from a low minimum wage and massive cuts in health, housing, education, and social insurance.

To convince the public that it stood to gain from a smaller government and weaker social programs, the reformers had to undermine the longstanding belief that government should play a large role in society. To this end, they equated tax-and-spend policies with big government and portrayed popular movements as greedy "special interests" that wanted "too much democracy." Civil rights gains were called reverse discrimination and the victories of the women's and gay rights movements were seen as a threat to "family values."

Having set the stage, the welfare reformers began the attack on the welfare state by targeting AFDC, the most vulnerable and least popular welfare program. Drawing on social science theories that blamed poverty on the values and behavior of the poor, the reformers put forward the belief that social problems stemmed from a "culture of poverty" that promoted "defective" values and "deviant" behavior. The American Enterprise Institute, a conservative think tank in Washington, D.C., argued that "a substantial minority of the poor is suffering from something more than the low income familiar in family memory to most Americans. This new thing, which we have called behavioral dependency is more like an inability to cope."[6] Similarly, a 1994 report published by the Heritage Foundation, another conservative think-tank, claimed that while the United States may have conquered material poverty, the abundant "behavioral" poverty continued to grow "at an alarming pace." The report defined behavioral poverty as "a cluster of severe social pathologies including: an eroded work ethic and dependency, the lack of educational aspirations and achievement, an inability or unwillingness to control one's children, as well as increased single parenthood, illegitimacy, criminal activity, and drug and alcohol use."[7]

Other conservatives blamed society's problems on social programs that they said created a "culture of entitlements." In 1987, the Reagan Administration had argued that "the easy availability of welfare in all of its forms has become a powerful force for the destruction of family life through the perpetuation of a welfare culture" that discourages work and marriage, creates an unhealthy sense of entitlement, promotes dependence, and encourages people to challenge authority." In 1994, the Cato Institute, a Libertarian research center, held that "children growing up in the welfare-ravaged neighborhoods...are the true victims of our social welfare policies." Many, like Charles Murray co-author of The Bell Curve, a controversial book that argues for the role of genetics in determining intelligence, took special aim at welfare. Murray recommended that "the AFDC payment go to zero," and that single mothers should not be eligible for subsidized housing, food stamps, or any other benefits.[8]

Some reformers fueled hostility to the welfare state by playing the race card. They implied that most poor people came from the African-American community, when in fact, more whites—reflecting their predominance in the population—than blacks live in poverty. Nor did they challenge the portrayal of welfare as an African-American program, even though government data showed that by the early 1980s the proportion of blacks and whites on welfare had both fallen and converged. By 1995, prior to the passage of TANF, blacks represented 37.2 percent of all AFDC cases, down from 44 percent in 1983. The white rate fell from 42 percent in 1983 to 36.6 percent in 1995. The major growth in the welfare rolls during this period took place among Latinos.[9] These negative images of poor blacks and the insidious messages about the culture, personal traits, and experiences of welfare recipients helped turn public opinion against welfare. Indeed, whites who believed that black people made up more than half of the poor favored cutting welfare spending more than whites who did not.[10] Since 1996, the work-first emphasis of welfare reform has tilted the racial composition of the rolls back toward women of color.[11] While both white women and women of color have moved off welfare in large numbers, white women who do not face racial discrimination have moved off the rolls more quickly.

Finally, by muddying the meaning of the term welfare, the campaigners spread the hostility they had stimulated toward AFDC to other social programs. Most specifically, and in this book, the word welfare refers to the public assistance program for single mothers and their children (AFDC/TANF). But social commentators also use the word to refer (1) to *all* the public assistance programs, (2) to *both* public assistance for the poor and social insurance for the middle class, (3) and, even more loosely, to public assistance, social insurance, and social programs in general. The multiple uses of the same word created considerable confusion, readily exploited by those who wanted to shelve all of the programs. When talking about the cost of "welfare" for single mothers, for example, some critics cited dollar figures inclusive of the other "welfare" programs. Having rallied support for axing the smaller welfare program because it cost too much, opponents of government programs simply referred to Medicare, Medicaid, Food Stamps, Social Security, and other popular programs as "welfare" and called for their retrenchment too.

Although this conservative analysis eventually held sway, others existed. Historically, liberals and radicals offered alternative understandings of the welfare state. The liberal philosophy, which underlay the development of the welfare state from the 1930s through the mid-1970s, reflected a positive view of government. Liberals believed that social problems arise from flaws in societal institutions (i.e. labor markets, barriers to health care) not from flawed individuals or overly permissive social programs; and that living and working in an industrial society leaves people vulnerable to loss of income due to old age, joblessness, illness, or family dissolution. Social welfare programs become both necessary and appropriate to protect people against adverse social and economic conditions. Prior to welfare reform, liberals had called for higher benefits, more responsive services, and less punitive rules. They wanted to follow the pattern set by other Western nations that defined social protections as the universal right of all members of a society—although in these countries too, welfare programs have come under attack.

Radicals, who look more closely at the workings of the economy, argued that poverty represents an inevitable feature of profit-driven economies based on private ownership of the means of production and the exploitation of labor. Thus, social problems stem from societal structures and the unequal distribution of money and power—not from individual behavior or malfunctioning institutions. However, when proposing remedies, not all radicals call for government programs. Some radicals believe that welfare programs control clients, cool-out protest movements, and co-opt the working class.[12] Others argue that social programs provide an economic boost that, if substantial enough, can increase the political leverage of marginalized groups. Access to alternative sources of income can help workers take the risks needed to resist exploitation on the job and help women to resist subordination in the home. Without denying its role in social control, these radicals see the welfare state as an arena for progressive political struggle between the haves and have-nots.[13]

THE LATEST WAR ON WELFARE:
WELFARE REFORM IN THE 1980S AND 1990S

FUELED BY THE DICTATES OF THE ECONOMIC RECOVERY plan, conservative analysis of social programs, and a dislike of govenment programs, the attack on welfare included five targets: the cost and size of AFDC, women's work behavior, women's childbearing choices, the entitlement status of social programs, and the overall role of the federal government in society.

The first edition of this book was written just before Congress passed the 1996 welfare reform law and could only anticipate its outcome. At that time, most advocates saw the proposed changes as a serious threat to poor families, public assistance, and the wider welfare state. Drawing on personal reports of the women forced to leave welfare and on the early research findings that

detail the outcome of welfare reform, this updated edition unfortunately only confirms advocates' worst fears. In too many cases welfare reform translates into increased stress, hardship, and poverty for poor women leading many commentators to ask: from welfare to what?

CUTTING THE COST AND SIZE OF WELFARE

THE FIRST ASSAULT ON THE WELFARE STATE BEGAN IN the early 1980s and emphasized the cost and size of its programs. The unpopularity of AFDC and its constituents—poor single mothers—made welfare an easy target for Ronald Reagan's economic recovery plan. The Administration's budget cutters argued that AFDC wasted funds on undeserving women and bloated bureaucracies; that it drained the treasury and fueled the deficit. They also insisted that women on welfare live "high on the hog." Yet the facts suggest otherwise. The average benefit rose from $178 a month in 1970, to $275 in 1980.[14] During the same time, however, due to inflation, its real purchasing power fell more than 40 percent. In no state did the combined value of the meager AFDC and Food Stamps grant lift a family of three above the official poverty line. Advocates of the poor called for higher AFDC benefits as part of the 1988 Family Support Act, but their proposal did not survive the political process.

While the cost of AFDC had indeed grown over the years, it could hardly be held responsible for the budget deficit or the nation's economic woes. In fact, it amounted to only 1.1 percent of the federal budget; 3.0 percent including the cost of Food Stamps (FS) and Supplemental Security Income (SSI). The state paid additional shares for AFDC. In contrast, a much larger 20.3 percent of the federal budget went to Social Security and 28 percent to military spending.

The federal share of AFDC costs rose to $14 billion in 1995, but fell to 0.9 percent of the federal budget; 4.5 percent including FS and SSI. That year Social Security took 22 percent and defense absorbed 18.5 percent. As for bureaucratic costs, benefits amounted to 88 percent of the $14 billion spent for AFDC in 1995, administration, only 12 percent.[15] Overall welfare spending fell far below the approximately $104 billion devoted to subsidies and tax breaks for U.S. corporations—or what some refer to as "corporate welfare."[16] In addition, the beneficiaries of the Food Stamps, Medicaid, and housing programs included some agriculture, medical, and real estate interests.

The myths surrounding welfare's size matched the misperceptions of its cost. By the late 1970s, welfare's critics told us that the rolls had exploded and created an uncontrollable mess. But AFDC's expansion mirrored social forces over which individuals typically have little or no control. The welfare rolls grew steadily during the late 1940s and 1950s, serving from 1 to 2 million individuals a year. The numbers doubled from about 3.0 million in 1960 to 10.2

million in 1971 reflecting high poverty rates but also the demands of the civil rights and welfare rights movements.[17] Even so, AFDC's expansion kept pace with natural population increases serving a steady 2 to 3 percent of all Americans until 1969, when it jumped to more than 4 percent. From 1971 to 1990, the caseload once again stabilized at 10 to 11 million people per year, or 4 to 5 percent of the U.S. population—except during recessions, when the numbers rose.[18]

Although welfare's growth reflected a normal response to population growth, fluctuating economic conditions, liberalized program rules, and pressure from social movements, critics used the convergence of three other developments to argue that welfare's expansion stemmed from the unacceptable values and behavior of the poor. In the 1970s, in some high-benefit states, the welfare grant began to exceed the minimum wage, making work less economically attractive than welfare for some women. This led critics to depict women on welfare as lazy. When the proportion of women of color, especially black women, peaked at 44 percent of the caseload, the condition of the program became racialized. And as single mothers replaced widows on the rolls, critics said welfare fueled immorality.

Drawing on these negative stereotypes, the newly elected Reagan Administration justified its deep cuts in welfare by arguing that denying poor women welfare would force them to mend their ways. Beginning in the 1980s, lawmakers cut welfare by tightening eligibility rules, lowering benefits, and defunding a host of social programs. The changes pushed thousands of women off the rolls into low-paid jobs, but also into dangerous welfare hotels, drug-plagued streets, and unsafe relationships. Congress also encouraged the states to experiment with stiff welfare-to-work programs which paved the way for the 1988 Family Support Act (FSA). The FSA transformed AFDC from a program to help single mothers stay home with their children into a mandatory work program. Blaming welfare's size and cost on the values and behavior of the poor, lawmakers hid the real agenda of welfare reform:

supplying business with more low-paid labor, shrinking the welfare state, and stigmatizing single motherhood.

By the end of the 1980s, the welfare rolls began to rise again. The upward drift reflected both the economy's poor health (stagnating wages, corporate downsizing, high unemployment) and rising poverty stemming from economic decline and the massive cuts in social programs for the poor. By 1994, the welfare caseload reached a new high of 14.2 million individuals or 5.5 percent of the entire population.[19] By then, more politicians had latched onto the welfare issue for political gain. Indeed President Clinton and many others won office in 1992 by promising "to end welfare as we know it."

Much to everyone's surprise, shortly after the implementation of TANF, the national welfare rolls plummeted from 14.2 million people 1994 to 7.6 million in December 1998—or more than 40 percent.[20] The importance of these rapid and steep declines cannot be downplayed, but they do not tell the whole story of welfare reform in America. A closer look suggests that the falling welfare rolls once again reflected systemic forces: an improved economy, newly restrictive program rules, and weakened social movements. It also appears that those who proclaimed welfare reform a success did so without questioning the impact on the women who left the rolls.

The booming economy clearly helped welfare to shrink. It is no trick to reduce the welfare rolls in a period of near full-employment, soaring stock markets, and general prosperity. Presented with more jobs, labor shortages, and higher wages, women typically leave welfare if they can. But a healthy economy does not represent a permanent fix. Indeed most economists predict the next recession will erase many of the current gains causing the welfare rolls to rise again. No doubt welfare's critics will once again call women on welfare lazy and unmotivated for work.

Nor is it a trick to lower the welfare rolls by refusing to help women and children in crisis. TANF resurrected two of the oldest and most discredited methods of limiting welfare's cost and size:

deterrence and punishment. Deterrence has taken several forms. First, critics intensified the rhetoric stigmatizing welfare receipt, leading fewer people to apply. Second, TANF rewarded states financially for reducing their rolls and for placing women in work activities. Third, more than half the states have established formal diversion programs to avoid enrolling families on welfare. Diversion programs require caseworkers to press poor women to ask family and friends for help, to take a one-time, lump sum payment instead of an ongoing grant, and to engage in job search activities prior to filling out an application.[21] They subject applicants to excessively long waits and unnecessary return visits in hopes that they will give up and go away. If these tactics do not work, welfare departments encourage caseworkers to find ways to deprive applicants of information about the full range of benefits available to them and to otherwise find ways to reject rather than process applications. A New Jersey woman told researchers, "Yeah, the workers really make things harder. They don't go out of their way to tell you about stuff, give you information about program, and you know they look for every excuse to cut somebody off and limit their income."[22] Massachusetts's researchers found that 40 percent of their respondents did not know that welfare covered childcare costs for one year after they left the program. Huge declines in New York City's Medicaid and Food Stamp rolls led advocates to sue the city for failing to inform applicants about their eligibility for these programs and to a federal investigation into the city's welfare practices.

Deterrence politics have a long history, resurfacing in conservative political periods. But they cannot keep everyone away. Therefore, the states have also increased the use of punitive penalties to lower their rolls. Prior to TANF, Federal rules hampered states from cutting off families for failure to work. Now caseworkers must sanction anyone who fails to cooperate with the new work rules, regardless of their circumstances. "I have been very nervous," explained a New Jersey recipient: "I'm afraid that if I do not follow every order and command that I am given, I'll be cut off. The process becomes extremely stressful." A mother of twins in Columbus, Ohio with serious asthma and depression reported: "I still have to get a job or they are going to cut me. They told me there are no excuses."[23] A Memphis women with recurring back pain lost her grant for missing her training classes and showing up late for an appointment with her caseworker. In Utah, half the sanctioned families had identifiable problems that caseworkers ignored. In some states, more people left welfare due to sanctions than to successful job hunting.[24] As if these sanctions were not enough, Michigan became the first state to pass legislation mandating drug tests for welfare recipients and applicants. Those who fail the test must enter a drug treatment program and face loss of benefits if they do not comply with its rules.[25]

ENFORCING THE WORK ETHIC

THE SECOND ATTACK ON WELFARE TRAINED ITS SIGHTS on women's work behavior. It meshed with efforts of Presidents Reagan, Bush, and Clinton to promote economic growth by lowering labor costs for employers. Indeed, TANF's "work-first" policy flooded the labor market with thousands of workers. The increased competition for jobs pressed wages down and made it harder for unions to negotiate good contracts.

From 1935 until the late 1960s, society expected women, especially mothers of young children, to stay home—although poverty prevented women from following this advice. Official welfare policy, which incorporated this gender norm, penalized recipients if they went to work. Of course, welfare departments regularly skirted the federal guidelines by setting benefits lower than wages, restricting eligibility, and otherwise servicing local employers who wanted poor women to fill low-paying jobs.

By the mid-1970s, social attitudes toward women's work had changed. The feminist movement encouraged women to seek greater independence by earning their own way. At the same time, the demand for female workers grew in response to both the rapid expansion of low-paid service jobs typically reserved for women and the fears of business and industry that labor shortages in the service sector would lower their profits by pushing wages up. Some business experts predicted that by the year 2000, labor markets would be "tighter than at any time in recent history."[26] During this period, rising welfare grants in the higher benefit states made it economically rational for some women to choose welfare over work.

Rather than try to attract women workers by addressing their concerns about unequal pay, health benefits, and family responsibilities, business urged government to consider welfare reform. In 1986, the National Alliance of Business (NAB) concluded, "welfare recipients represent an important source of needed workers" that must be "encouraged to enter the labor market through government-subsidized education, training, and social services."[27] The 1988 Family Support Act introduced the Job Opportunity and Basic Security (JOBS) program, which required recipients to work, search for a job, or participate in education and training programs. To maintain their federal matching funds, the states had to enroll 15 percent of their AFDC caseload in a JOBS program by 1995. The JOBS program also extended childcare services and Medicaid coverage for one year to ease the transition from welfare to training and employment. These supports helped women take the jobs business needed to fill. They also eliminated the pressure on business to provide these benefits to attract and hold onto workers. The FSA's acceptance of education as work preparation also suited business. The NAB observed: "No sector [of the economy] can afford a growing underclass that cannot get or keep jobs, nor can the nation afford to suffer losses in productivity and world competitiveness because workers are unprepared for changes in the workplace."[28] As if in response, the FSA allowed states to count women attending literacy, GED, and undergraduate college programs as work participants which qualified the states for federal funds.

The dramatic conversion of welfare from a program that allowed single mothers to stay home with their children into a mandatory work program in the late 1980s led most observers to believe that the twenty-year effort to revamp welfare had ended.

Thus Clinton surprised nearly everyone when, in 1992, he proposed to transform AFDC into a transitional and temporary work program. If the assault on welfare's size and cost depended on misinformed explanations of welfare's growth, the push for a more intense work program drew on myths about women, welfare, and work—in particular the portrayal of women on welfare as lazy and unmotivated. For example, Lawrence Mead, a conservative political scientist, concluded "the poor remain economically passive in a society where other low-skilled people find abundant opportunity." Governor Kirk Fordice of Mississippi told a reporter that "the only job training that welfare recipients need is a good alarm clock."[29] Only the strong arm of the government would cause women on welfare to change their ways.

Those who accepted these myths ignored massive amounts of contradictory evidence. For years researchers had reported that more than half of all single mothers on welfare had a prior work history, had worked while receiving benefits, and left the rolls within two years in response to the availability of decent paying jobs with adequate transportation, child care and health benefits.[30] The Washington-based Institute For Women's Policy Research, found that "recipients use AFDC for many reasons, including to supplement their low-wage work effort and to provide a safety net during periods of unemployment, disability, and family crises."[31] A decade of scientifically respected evaluations had also found that most of the 1980's welfare-to-work experiments had yielded only modest employment results.[32]

Passed in August 1996, the new federal welfare law known as TANF was implemented in most states within a year. Reflecting the "work first" approach, TANF placed a lifetime limit of five years on welfare eligibility (less at state option). Despite the widely known research findings noted above, the 1996 law also stiffened the FSA's already strict work mandates. TANF insisted that within five years one-half of a state's welfare caseload must be enrolled in job or job-search activity for up to 35 hours a week—or lose federal funding. Yet most states had failed to meet the much lower participation rate mandated by the FSA. In addition, welfare recipients who do not find work must "work off" their benefits by cleaning parks and offices for public or private agencies, without any employee benefits or protections.[33] TANF also made it more difficult for poor women to escape poverty through additional training and education by excluding college education from the list of work and training activities that qualify states for funding. Many women have had to leave school, including college, for dead-end work programs or low-wage jobs.

Meanwhile, business took another look at the welfare which now allowed the states to privatize some programs. At a March 1997 conference, business leaders learned that TANF represented: "the business opportunity of a lifetime;" how to "gain a leading edge in the market while it in its early stage," and how to "capitalize on the massive growth potential of the new world of welfare reform." Lockheed and IBM competed heavily for the $2 billion contract to run the entire eligibility process for TANF, Food Stamps, Medicaid, and other programs in Texas.[34] In 39 states major banks now manage the electronic banking card system used to distribute welfare benefits to the nation's poor. The banks profit by, among other means, assessing ATM fees on welfare recipients that regular ATM customers do not have to pay.[35]

As noted above, the stiff work-first rules combined with a strong economy caused a sharp drop in the welfare rolls. The early reports indicated that around 50 percent of the former recipients found work. However, the other 50 percent did not,[36] despite a 4.2 unemployment rate—the lowest since the 1960s. And this does not include those people that the researchers failed to locate. The welfare "reformers" insist that work empowers poor women, raises their self-esteem, and improves their economic circumstances. Without denying this, the mayor of Philadelphia explained, that "it is too much to expect that these numbers of welfare recipients are going to find jobs in these markets."[37]

Of the recipients that did find work, many simply joined the ranks of the working poor—earning between $6.00 and $8.00 an hour. The former recipients told researchers that due to low wages they could no longer make ends meet.[38] Their wages exceeded the $5.15 an hour minimum wage, but this did not lift their families out of poverty. The proportion of recipients with wages above the three-person poverty line rose slightly from 6 percent in 1990 to 8 percent in 1998. Meanwhile the number of those with weekly wages below three-quarters of the poverty line surged upward from 6 percent to 14.5 percent.[39] A welfare mother in Oregon concluded that pushing mothers off welfare into low-paid jobs may benefit businesses and politicians, but keeps women in "their place."[40]

Life for many former recipients has, if anything, worsened. A New Jersey women commented: "How are you supposed to survive on the minimum wage—feed the kids, pay the rent, utilities?[41] A summary of studies completed in nine states supports her concerns. It found that once off welfare 50 percent of the women studied found themselves behind in rent or utility payments, compared to 39 percent while on welfare. Fourteen percent said they now could not afford to pay for medical care, versus 3 percent before. Sixteen percent reported periods without enough money to buy food, compared to 7 percent while a welfare recipient.[42] Until the mid-1970s, a full-time, year-round job paying the federal minimum wage lifted a family out of poverty. Since that period, the wage floor has fallen further below the poverty line every year. Thus, eight years into an economic boom, the income of the bottom fifth has declined steadily, from 5.4 percent of the national total in 1979, to 4.6 percent in 1989, to 4.2 percent in 1997. Real buying power fell below 1979 levels.[43]

In addition to below-poverty wages, welfare reform cost many women access to Food Stamps, Medicaid and low-rent housing. In some cases, welfare failed to provide the promised transitional medical and childcare services needed by women to get and keep a job. Other women simply lost prior benefits. "I was worse off when I was working than I am now," explained a Massachusetts woman: "My food stamps stopped the first week of working and they were going to take my Medicaid away. Plus I had to pay for

part of the costs of childcare. My rent went up from $34 a month to $109. My highest check was $100 for a week, so one whole check would have to go for rent."[44] Human service workers report that families leaving welfare show more signs of homelessness and hunger and make greater use of shelters, food pantries, and child welfare services. Other service providers find that informal business—braiding hair, selling fruit by the roadside, providing in-home childcare—which formerly supplemented welfare checks have become the sole source of cash for some families. Still other observers fear that destitution will force more women into illegal activities such as drug trafficking and prostitution.[45]

Because the studies tracking women who leave welfare rarely reach the jobless women and the most troubled families, the findings barely capture the true hardship of women no longer on welfare. We do know, however, that the number of children living below *one-half the poverty line* for a family of three (or less than

$6,401 as a yearly income in 1997) grew by 400,000 between 1995 and 1997. We also know that one out of five children who live in poverty face a greater chance of having stunted growth, less education, and lower projected earnings then children raised above the poverty line. Statisticians trace much of the nationwide rise in poverty directly to the loss of government benefits.[46] Living in the gap between the haves and the have nots, many families report increased anxiety and stress. Since December 1, 1998, when Massachusetts began time limits, social workers have noticed increased instability in every aspect of low-income family life.[47]

Welfare reform also affects community life adversely. In the absence of jobs and decent pay, welfare dollars kept local merchants afloat in lower income communities. The merchants, in turn, hired local residents, made streets safer, and otherwise sustained the neighborhood's viability. Welfare reform has reduced the amount of cash flowing into poor communities, draining the last bit of money out of places abandoned by business and industry during the last 25 years for cheaper labor elsewhere. The nation's cities feel the negative impact of welfare reform in still another way. Already home to most of the nation's poverty and unemployment, they now find themselves serving a larger share of the national and state welfare population—even though the absolute numbers have dropped.[48] The mounting human and economic costs have begun to wreak havoc with the lives of people in these areas, the social service systems they rely on, as well as city and state budgets. A Kellogg Foundation study found that since TANF, community-based agencies have had more trouble doing their jobs due to increased caseloads; more emergency requests for food, housing, and utilities; and more people with drug, mental health, or other complex problems.[49]

In the past, when the economy failed poor women, they could turn to welfare until their circumstances improved or they could combine work with some welfare aid. But lifetime limits on welfare eligibility effectively eliminates this option. In those states that imposed a two-year time limit, thousands of women have already exhausted their benefits forever. By 2002, the five-year cap will take effect in all states. A former recipient noted, "They should not have a five-year time limit on people who are not able to get on their feet right away. You could get hurt or sick, then what? They should look at each situation. Every situation is different."[50] Time limited welfare ignores important realities: some women cannot work outside the home due to ill health, low education, lack of skills, disabilities, emotional problems, or other barriers to employment. Another reality is that the labor market rarely has room for all those ready and able to work.

By 1999, many states had tightened the TANF screws. However, in some states, welfare rights and advocacy groups have successfully pressured legislatures to make small changes. Aimed at facilitating employment, some states have stopped the time limit clock for working families, expanded childcare services, extended the earned income disregard for the working poor; exempted recipients in education and training programs from time limits and reduced their work requirement hours, enacted state Earned Income Tax Credits to supplement the federal program, increased the public assistance grant, and created public job creation programs.[51]

In most cases, the states that made these positive changes utilized unspent TANF funds. The dollars became available because in 1996 TANF funded the states at a fixed level for five years (1997–2002) based on the size of their 1994 caseload. With the sudden drop in the rolls, the states found themselves with extra money to spend. A few states used the windfall to raise benefit levels. A larger number created new services for welfare recipients. However, many states have used the federal dollars in ways that did not benefit women on welfare. They reimbursed previous state spending on existing welfare benefits and services, expanded services (such as childcare) for the working poor, and even funded a tax cut for the well-to-do. A third group of states either saved some of the funds for a "rainy day" or did not spend the money at all.[52] Some in Congress see the unused dollars as an opportunity to build a case for reducing federal welfare spending in 2002, when funding for the current welfare law expires. In contrast, advocates for the poor continue to argue that "real" reform means creating jobs that pay a living wage and providing guaranteed adequate cash assistance for those not in the labor market. These policies need not be beyond the reach of the richest country in the world.

UPHOLDING THE FAMILY ETHIC

A THIRD PART OF THE ASSAULT ON POOR WOMEN AND welfare took aim at women's marital, childbearing, and parenting behavior. This attack enforced the family values agenda pushed by the new right since the early 1980s, if not before, and included in the ongoing economic recovery plan. Like the work ethic, welfare reform also embodies the "family ethic"—a set of beliefs holding that everyone should marry and live in two-parent, heterosexual households, preferably with one wage earner and one home-maker.[53] With this narrow version of "family" in mind, in the late 1980s, the New Right declared that the family, as they defined it, was imperiled by the rise of working wives, single mothers, divorced couples, gay parents, interracial marriages, test-tube babies, legalized abortion, birth control, the sexual revolution— and *government welfare programs*.[54]

Responding to these concerns, the 1996 welfare reform law sought "to stigmatize single motherhood and to encourage the formation and maintenance of two-parent families."[55] TANF furthered this goal with harsh penalties for women who departed from prescribed wife and mother roles. Some critics think of these efforts to control the behavior of poor women as economic coercion because they force women in dire financial circumstances to trade their health, contraceptive, religious, and parenting preferences for a welfare check. The racial stereotypes about women of color as matriarchal, hypersexed, and promiscuous, which lurk just below the surface of these policies, cannot be missed. Yet recent data shows that while black women still have higher rates of single motherhood and nonmarital births than white women, the disparity by race on both these measures has lessened due to declining rates among blacks and rising rates among whites.[56]

CHILDBEARING

TANF REACHED DEEP INTO FAMILY LIFE WITH THE HIGHLY controversial child exclusion, also called the family cap. Aimed at stopping welfare recipients from having additional children, it allows the states to deny increased cash aid to women who conceive and bear another child while on welfare. Although protests by both feminists and anti-abortion groups caused Congress not to require the states to adopt the child exclusion, more than 23 of them took the option by February 1999.[57]

TANF also contains what it calls the "illegitimacy" bonus which provides large cash rewards of 20 to 25 billion dollars to the states that reduce their nonmarital birth and their abortion rates statewide, not just for women on welfare.[58] Finally TANF earmarks $250 billion in matching funds for states that run "abstinence-only" programs in public schools. By March 1999, every state, except California had accepted these funds for programs which stress abstinence and sex within marriage.[59] Fearing that this will radically alter how the nation's public schools teach sex education, five national health education organizations have pressed Congress to replace the provision with "effective sexuality education that is part of a comprehensive school health education." Reproductive control of women on welfare takes still other forms. Colorado lawmakers considered penalizing welfare recipients who refused family planning counseling. Utah officials thought about paying $3,000 to unwed pregnant women who carried their babies to term and put them up for adoption.[60] Some state have encouraged recipients to use Norplant (the long lasting contraceptive implant) while others have allocated TANF funds for more general family planning programs.[61]

Social conservatives promote these policies to control the reproductive choices of women on welfare. Holding welfare responsible for rising rates of non-marital births among poor women, Charles Murray called "illegitimacy" the "single most important social problem of our time—more important than crime, drugs, poverty, illiteracy, welfare, or homelessness—because it drives everything else." He concluded that single mothers drain community resources, destroy the community's capacity to sustain itself, and should therefore not be given economic support.[62] The conservatives also believe that welfare encourages women to have large families as a way to increase their welfare grant.

Critics of the child exclusion argue that the data presents a different picture. Since 1975, the average welfare family has included only two children, the same as the national rate. In 1995, 73 percent of women on welfare had one or two children, up from 63 percent in 1973 and 49 percent in 1969. In 1995, less than 10 percent of women on welfare had four or more children.[63] Since a woman must have at least one child to qualify for welfare and since most women have only one more child while on the rolls, welfare can hardly be considered to cause large families.

The critics also argue that access to cash benefits does not create incentives to procreate. Even before the child exclusion denied benefits altogether, the welfare grant for additional children included barely enough to pay for milk and diapers, much less influence childbearing decisions. Moreover, few people would claim that the current U.S. income tax exemption for dependents, the Earned Income Tax Credit, or the childcare tax credit for mothers who stay home invite women to have additional children. That many women at all income levels have an unintended pregnancy further suggests the futility of bonuses and penalties.[64]

Trend data also suggest that access to welfare benefits do not cause nonmarital births which now represent 32 percent of all U.S. births, mostly to women between age 18 and 29, not teens.[65] In fact, states with higher benefits do not necessarily have higher nonmarital or teenage birth rates and vice versa. From 1971 to 1996 the overall nonmarital birth rate rose steadily while the real

value of the welfare check plummeted from $774 to $397 (in 1996 dollars). Moreover the growing population of unmarried mothers includes many women not on welfare. Finally, despite more generous benefits, European nations have far lower teenage birth rates than the U.S.[66]

The implementation of the child exclusion provided the opportunity to study its impact on childbearing behavior. Much to the chagrin of its proponents, researchers reported that the punitive measure does not work. Arkansas, which instituted the child exclusion experimentally prior to the federal welfare reform, found no difference in birth rates between women subject to the child exclusion and a control group. The New Jersey experiment led to a 140 percent decline in the birth rate from 1993 to 1996. But most of the fall stemmed from a 240 percent increase in the abortion rate among women on welfare. Meanwhile, the overall abortion rate in both New Jersey and the nation dropped. We do not know what happened to the more than 25,000 New Jersey children denied assistance under this rule.[67] But child-protection officials openly fear that welfare reform will flood the child welfare system with childen whose parents can no longer provide or care for them.[68]

MARRIAGE

BENEATH THE CONCERN ABOUT SINGLE MOTHERHOOD lies the fear that government programs, especially welfare for single mothers, discourage marriage and cause families to "breakdown." In the mid-1990s, Robert Rector, a social analyst for the Heritage Foundation declared: "Across the nation, the current welfare system has all but destroyed family structure in low-income communities." "Welfare" he continued, "established strong financial incentives which effectively block the formation of intact, two-parent families....Largely because of welfare, illegitimacy and single parenthood have now become the conventional lifestyle option for raising children in many low-income communities."[69] Stuart Butler and Anna Kondratas, two other conservative commentators, charged that AFDC financed "a subculture of people" who want children but not marriage, who disdain family commitments, and "who downplay the importance of male figures." The typical AFDC parent today, they say, is not the worthy widow envisaged in the original legislation but the divorced, deserted, or never-married woman. In this view, any family without a father is defective: "Raised in an environment in which fathers don't provide for the young and dependency on government is assumed, few children will develop the skills of self-sufficiency, or even the concept of personal responsibility. Young men will not strive to be good providers, and young women will not expect it of their men."[70] Reflecting these views, welfare policy penalizes single motherhood. A few states have introduced a marriage bonus: higher benefits for some two-parent households on welfare.

Welfare may disqualify most two-parent families. But it does not create single-parent households. Indeed, research, psychology, and plain common sense suggest that even poor people marry and divorce for a host of reasons unrelated to welfare. Life stresses frequently weigh heavily on marriage, stresses that poverty can only compound. Testifying at a public hearing, a recipient explained:

"My recent marriage broke up over financial stress. My husband is in and out of work (mostly out) and we simply could not handle the stress of no money and his not working."[71] When low wages and high unemployment prevent men from carrying out their breadwinner roles, fewer men and women want to, or can, marry. This is especially true for African Americans when racism takes a heavy toll on male employment. Of course, regardless of race not all women choose to marry. Nor is marriage necessarily an effective anti-poverty strategy. While two earners live better than one, many women remain poor even after they tie the knot: two-earner households represent one of the nation's fastest growing poverty groups.

The national data on families suggest that forces other than welfare have led to the rise of single motherhood. From 1970 to 1997, the number of female-headed householders increased by 133 percent (from 5.5 million to 12.8 million) while the value of the welfare grant declined. The proportion of single-parent families rose from 11 percent of all families with children under 18 in 1970 to 24 percent in 1990 to 28 percent in 1997. Most of these households do not receive welfare. Meanwhile, the percentage of all two-parent families fell from 89 to 75 to 72 percent. While more black women than white women become single mothers, since 1980 the numbers fell among blacks, but reached new heights among whites. In 1997, due to their larger numbers in the U.S. population, whites made up 63 percent of all female-headed households.[72]

Ignoring these trends, Heather Mac Donald from the conservative Manhattan Institute believes that all social programs should "reward marriage not illegitimacy." She urged New York City to give "preference to married families in the distribution of public housing, explicitly articulating its reasons for doing so." Mac Donald also opposes public day care programs, which she thinks give priority to "parents who have abused their children, teen mothers, and homeless families." In her mind all of these groups represent "near stand-ins for single parents."[73]

PARENTING

SOME WELFARE REFORM PROVISIONS ALSO TARGET POOR women's parenting. The view of single-parent families as "broken" or "deviant" reflects the long-standing distrust of women who raise children without men, especially poor, nonwhite, or foreign-born women. According to Myron Magnet also of the Manhattan Institute "anyone who looks at underclass children—neglected, abused, unimmunized, deprived of the moral and cognitive nurturing that families provide—has to ask whose welfare is advanced by a system that consigns so many children to emotional and intellectual stunting and to likely failure in school and later life." From the child's point of view, he added, "an incompetent mother on crack is not better than a Dickensian orphanage." Magnet favors placing poor children and their mothers in group homes that provide "the whole array of cognitive and moral categories that one is supposed to learn at home." Mac Donald, cited earlier, regularly reiterates Magnet's call.[74]

Americans have long expressed distrust in the parenting capacity of poor women. Throughout the twentieth century and before, officials regularly removed poor children from their homes to institutions. The lack of trust in poor women's ability to socialize their children—which must sound odd to the poor women hired to care for the children of middle- and upper-class families—underlies welfare reform proposals to reduce the benefits of welfare recipients. Only financial deprivation, it is believed, will motivate welfare recipients to parent "responsibly." Thus Learnfare docks the welfare checks of mothers with truant children and Healthfare lowers the grant of mothers who do not have their children immunized on schedule.

The value of school attendance and doctor visits goes without saying. Learnfare, however, ignores its own evaluator's conclusion that "a troubling large number of teens described their schools as dangerous and frightening places where learning was difficult." The report recommended educational as well as welfare reform.[75]

The Healthfare advocates downplay the lack of medical services in poor neighborhoods. Improving the public schools and providing access to healthcare would help poor parents far more than welfare's behavior modification approach. When parents do need guidance, positive outreach works more effectively than threats of punishment by the state.

The campaign to wring child support from "deadbeat dads" targets the parenting behavior of poor men. Stiffer paternity and child-support rules require states to reduce benefits for women who refuse to identify their child's father. Likewise for those who cooperate but fail to establish paternity even if the reason is bureaucratic red tape or the father's ability to conceal his whereabouts. Twenty states reduce the benefit by more than the 25 percent minimum. Another thirteen states eliminate benefits entirely.[76]

The reformers believe that the vigorous child-support requirements will turn non-paying fathers into responsible providers and reduce welfare costs. Critics claim that while known paternity helps children gain access to child support and Social Security survivor's benefits, the effort often yields only a few dollars because poor women often partner with poor men. They also fear that the push for child support may jeopardize relationships that many poor men, sometimes with difficulty, maintain with their children on welfare. Aggressive pursuit of child support can, they say, also expose women to male violence. To many advocates, the real purpose of the crackdown is to teach "deadbeat dads" a lesson about personal responsibility and to castigate single mothers for raising children on their own.

Welfare reform's ostensible concern about parenting has not translated into policies that help poor women take care of their kids. Originally designed to enable single mothers to stay home, welfare once represented a partial acknowledgment of the important and time-consuming role of parenting. In contrast, TANF's time limits, stiff work rules, and heavy sanctions devalue women's caretaking work. They also make it harder for poor women to supervise their children effectively, especially in neighborhoods plagued by drugs, crime, and violence. A New Jersey welfare mother who could not find childcare for her ten-year-old son explained: " So he comes home to an empty house. . . . I don't like to admit it because I don't think a ten- year-old should be left home alone, but I don't have a choice. . . . Summer is a very hard time for me, I have nothing to do with him. . . . I worry about him all day."[76] Another New Jersey welfare mom reported that "I almost quit my job because of my kids. I want to keep working but I want my kids involved in activities too." She took a six-month break because "I was depressed. I just couldn't do everything with the job and make sure the kids were taken care of." In the words of a Wisconsin welfare mother: "Even kids on welfare need their moms."[78]

Caring for kids cannot be easy for poor women who live on limited incomes and in neighborhoods with substandard housing, overpriced food, troubled schools, and inadequate access to health care, childcare and social services. Parenting becomes particularly time consuming in poor families where searching for free or low-cost goods and services can become a fulltime job. The welfare "reformers" downplay the burdens faced by poor woman trying to balance work and family responsibilities. Yet a January 1999 National Survey of Family Well-Being found that low-income families consistently experience greater strain than higher income households. They worry more about paying for food, mortgages, utilities, health care and have higher incidences of poor mental health, higher levels of aggravation, especially if a parent.[79] Sometimes the mounting stress of poverty can lead to battering, depression, child neglect, and child abuse. While many non-welfare mothers are able to manage the stress by working part-time, welfare reform sends single mothers on welfare to full-time jobs or work programs, ignoring how work affects their ability to respond to their children's need for time and attention. Few welfare evaluations ask women how they cope with sickness, unpaid bills, unsafe neighborhoods, kids who want brand names sneakers, men who do not pay child support, and the shame of having to ask friends and relatives for time and money over and over again. In the final analysis, women turn to welfare in order to better care for their children. As one New Jersey woman stated: "If it wasn't for the program, I don't know, what I'd do with the kids...No parent wants to sit back and let their children starve and go without clothing."[80]

ATTACKING ENTITLEMENTS

THE FOURTH ATTACK ON WELFARE ALSO MESHED WELL with the economic recovery plan begun in the early 1980s. By undercutting the principle of entitlement—the strongest feature of the U.S. social welfare system—it helped to weaken the welfare state and discredit the regulatory role of the federal government .

The notion of entitlement represents a philosophical commitment and a budgetary mechanism that places the government on the side of people in need. Since the 1930s, the federal government pledged responsibility for the general welfare of its citizens and provided regular and automatic funding for a group of programs called entitlements. In theory, as long as welfare fell into the entitlement category, no one who met the program's eligibility rules went without assistance. While many states historically denied or provided very low benefits to persons of color or otherwise manipulated the rules, the entitlement principle set a standard to be reached and enforced.[81]

When the PRA converted welfare from a federal entitlement program into a block grant administered by the states, it made one of the most far-reaching changes in U.S. social-welfare history since the passage of the 1935 Social Security Act. Once welfare lost its entitlement status, the federal guarantee of monies disappeared. No longer will federal welfare funding to the states automatically rise when inflation, recession, population growth, or other conditions intensify the demand. If the need for welfare in a state exceeds its resources, its lawmakers must now choose between unpopular options: raising taxes, cutting benefits, denying aid to the poor, creating a waiting list, or simply ending welfare.[82]

Moreover, the funding for TANF expires in the year 2002, at which time the program's future funding becomes subject to the highly politicized and uncertain congressional budget process.

By transforming welfare into a state-run block grant, Congress also fragmented an already decentralized system. Prior to TANF, states complied with federal guidelines in exchange for federal support. This created some uniformity while delegating considerable control to the states including the right to define "need," to set their own benefit levels, and to establish other rules. By honoring states' rights, the program created the space for discriminatory practices as noted above. It also resulted in interstate benefit differences that exceeded variations in the cost of living. In 1996, benefits ranged from a high of $923 a month in Alaska to a low of $120 a month in Mississippi. Now that states can use some TANF dollars for other than cash assistance, more state to state variation will occur.

Ending welfare as an entitlement poses a real threat to the economic security of poor women and children. But for those who oppose what they refer to as "big government," welfare reform represents the first step in a wider effort to dismantle the more popular social welfare programs serving the middle-class as well as the poor. The taboo against tampering with *any* entitlement program has been broken, which makes it that much easier to target others. Indeed, shortly after President Clinton signed the welfare reform bill which stripped AFDC of its entitlement status, the Commission on Social Security Reform recommended several ways to privatize Social Security—the nation's strongest and most universal income support program—previously believed to be politically untouchable. Since then Congress has been debating, not *if* but *how and when* to turn Social Security over to Wall Street and Medicare over to the private insurance companies.

The attack on the welfare state also helps to discredit the overall role of the federal government in society, another goal of the economic recovery program. President Clinton himself declared that "the era of big government is over." Once the government comes under this kind of political fire, it becomes that much easier to cut taxes and limit the ability of the government to protect consumers, workers and the environment; to regulate business practices, and to otherwise limit corporate America's already high profits. As this book went to press, the Supreme Court ruled in favor of three cases (unrelated to welfare) that "significantly strengthened the power of the states in the Federal system while weakening those of the Federal Government." The editors of the *New York Times* concluded that these "alarming decisions will make it harder to enforce uniform policies on matters of national concern like the environment or health."[83]

THE WAR ON WELFARE CONCERNS ALL WOMEN

WELFARE REFORM HARMS POOR WOMEN ON PUBLIC assistance first and foremost. But, it also threatens the right of *all* women to decent pay, to control their own sexuality, to live free of abusive relationships, and to survive in families that do not fit the two-parent model. Welfare reform does this by undercutting caretaking supports, reproductive rights, safety from male violence, and economic independence.

Caretaking supports: As with life insurance, women hope that they will never need it, but any woman can fall on hard times. Since welfare reform downplays the value of women's work, it undercuts the need to support women's caretaking activities in the home. By legitimizing social program cuts, welfare reform poses a threat to the economic resources of all families that rely on government dollars to help with the cost of housing, health care, childcare, elder care, family leave, and other services. Cutting these programs also shifts the costs of caretaking and homemaking from the government back to women in the home and increases the burden of those trying to balance work and family responsibilities. Depriving women of caretaking supports makes it harder for women to work outside the home, an outcome desired by family-values advocates for women—other than single mothers on welfare.

Reproductive rights: The attack on poor women's reproductive choices also undermines the reproductive rights of all women. The welfare reformers insist that poverty is caused by sex and childbearing rather than lack of skills, poor education, and low-paying jobs. In response, welfare reform tries to control women's reproductive choices. Once the government wins the right to deny aid to women who have children while on welfare and to otherwise limit the reproductive rights of poor women, it becomes that much easier to tamper with the reproductive rights of all women. The pattern already exists. Shortly after 1973, when the Supreme Count (in Roe v. Wade) granted women the right to an abortion, the right-to-life forces won passage of the Hyde Amendment, which forbids the use of Medicaid dollars for abortions. Since then, abortion foes have successfully limited the reproductive rights of women regardless of their economic class. Welfare reform follows suit.

Male Violence: Male violence poses a serious problem for women on and off welfare. Researchers estimate that from 50 to 65 percent of welfare recipients have experienced abuse. Feminists fought for the Family Violence Option in the 1996 welfare law to ensure that the states screen welfare recipients for battering, provide services, and waive work rules that would force women off welfare into abusive situations. Unfortunately, few states actively enforce these safeguards. A women is battered every fifteen minutes in the United States. Two to four million are battered every year. While not all battered women are poor or on welfare, adequate welfare provision makes it economically possible for any women to escape dangerous and exploitative relationships.

Economic independence: The attack on welfare threatens the economic independence of all women by making it harder to earn a living. First, a smaller welfare state means fewer of the public-sector jobs that enabled many women—both white women and women of color—to enter the middle class. Second, to the extent that time limits, work rules, and punitive sanctions increase the competition for low wage jobs, welfare reform presses wages down for all low-paid workers, both women and men. Finally, shrinking welfare benefits undercuts cash aid, which represents a potential economic backup for any woman. The economic security provided by such a fall back makes it easier for workers to fight exploitation on the job and harder for employers to keep workers in line. The security also permits women to take the risks associated with resisting male domination in the home.

WHY NOW?

WE HAVE SEEN THAT WELFARE REFORM HAS WREAKED havoc with women's lives and the wider welfare state. Drawing on myths about the relationship between welfare and women's work, marital, childbearing, and parenting behavior, today's welfare programs intensify the regulation of womens lives. Ignoring massive research findings, labor-market realities, and the dynamics of family life, welfare reformers attacked the program for single mothers and then interpreted declining welfare rolls as a success. However, welfare rights advocates maintain that welfare reform has failed because it has increased the economic vulnerability of many poor women, threatened the well-being of many of the non-poor, did little or nothing to help poor women and children escape poverty, and undercut the entire welfare state.

I have tried to show that welfare reform was neither accidental nor simply meanspirited. Rather it helped to carry out the well-known plan for economic recovery which increased the profits for those at the top by imposing austerity on nearly everyone else. Welfare reform helped lower labor costs, shrink the welfare state, enforce family values, and discredit the role of the federal government in wider society. Forcing women off welfare keeps wages down by expanding the supply of workers who must compete for low-paying jobs. Welfare reforms also threatened the wider welfare state by creating support for social program cuts and undermining the principle of entitlement. This disinvestment in social welfare reflected corporate America's abandonment of U.S.

workers and eased its fears that government spending competed for funds with private investment. By attacking social welfare programs, the nation's leaders also helped to discredit the federal government's protective and regulatory functions. In no small way, welfare reform enforced the family values agenda promulgated by the social conservatives who deplore not only single mothers but also homosexuality, sex education and the right to abortion.

The economic recovery plan initiated in the early 1980s also weakened the power of social movements that tried to resist this austerity plan. Social movements represent the interests of the more powerless members of society. During the years after the second World War, these movements gained members and influence by, among other things, winning a wide range of government benefits for their members and others. Like a strike fund, the availability of these benefits, especially unemployment insurance, welfare, and health insurance, also increased the movement's bargaining power with employers and with the government.

Ronald Reagan signaled the assault on social movements when he broke the air traffic controllers strike, attacked the gains of the civil rights movement, and became the first President to speak out against abortion. These actions let business and the wider public know that it was okay to "go after" the trade unions, civil rights, and women's movements which lost many of their hard-won gains. The losses placed the movements on the defensive, cost them members and deprived them of time, money, and energy needed to fight back, much less progress. However, the effort to silence protest never fully succeeded. Indeed activism, including social welfare activism has a long history in the United States. As detailed in Part 4, whenever the attacks occurred, poor, working and middle-class women fought back. The current assault on the welfare state is no exception. But first Part 2 looks at how and why welfare, as a program for single mothers, became especially vulnerable to attack.

PART TWO

A Program Just for Single Mothers

THE DRIVE TO "REFORM" WELFARE IS NOT NEW: IT IS SIMPLY the most recent in a long series of attacks on programs for the poor, in particular those serving impoverished women. Moreover, neither the target of the attacks nor the rhetoric surrounding them has changed much. This part will look at the history of efforts to reform public assistance: the end of "outdoor relief" in both the early and late 1800s; the creation of Mothers' Pensions in the early 1900s; the inclusion of AFDC as part of the 1935 Social Security Act; the restrictive AFDC policies imposed after World War II; and the crackdown that began in the late 1960s, won a small reprieve, and then continued into the 1980s. From the attack on colonial poor laws to the most recent assault, the critics of welfare have repeatedly targeted women's work and family structures. As with the most recent debate over welfare described in Part 1, in each earlier period welfare came under attack when the provision of relief and the needs of the labor market did not mesh, and when changes in family life threatened the patriarchal status quo.

ATTACKS ON PUBLIC AID IN THE EARLY NINETEENTH CENTURY

THE FIRST MAJOR ATTACK ON PUBLIC AID TOOK PLACE IN the 1820s, after a thirty-year economic boom and at a time when the Industrial Revolution was leading to vast transformations in work and family patterns. A growing landless population had gathered in the cities and towns, and the proportion of workers employed by others expanded from 12 percent in 1800 to 40 percent in 1860.[1] The emerging urban working class faced a new kind of poverty, one that stemmed less from lack of property, bad harvests, or physical disability than from low wages and irregular work. During this period, although the largest cities increased their per capita spending on the poor, local relief systems could not meet the demand. The indigent included many women: single women who had been "freed" by the decline of household production to labor in the new mills and "manufactories," and the wives of low, irregularly paid, or absent men. For example, in 1816, New York City reserved the majority of its relief baskets for women; they were marked with such notations as "husband in prison," "husband has broken leg," "husband bad fellow," and "husband has abandoned her and she has broken her arm."[2]

The existing system of public aid not only began to sag under the weight of the poverty created by the developing market economy, but its methods became both abusive and obsolete. For instance, town officials typically auctioned off the able-bodied poor to the highest bidder, contracted paupers out to local farmers, and barred indigent strangers who might require relief from settling in town. The relief programs relied on aiding people in their own or a neighbor's home and therefore suited an economy based on agricultural production. But because they kept people tied to their households and to the land, the programs interfered with the imperatives of the market economy, which increasingly depended on a mobile and docile labor force rather than independent farmers and artisans. Indeed, the new merchants complained that the poor laws diminished the work effort by "removing the dread of want" widely held to be the prime mover of the lower orders of society.[3] Nor did the existing system adequately reduce the social turmoil created by wage workers—both men and women—who were beginning to form labor associations and political parties to protect their interests.

Residents gather outside an almshouse on Blackwell's (now Roosevelt) Island, New York City, 1890. [Photo by Jacob A. Riis, from the Jacob A. Riis Collection, Museum of the City of New York.]

The market economy also placed new pressures on family life. For one, the Industrial Revolution and the growth of a waged labor force undercut traditional avenues of upward mobility, which had been based on land ownership, and stimulated travel in search of new opportunities. Such changes loosened family and community ties, weakened paternal control of the home, diminished the family's central role in governing community affairs, and in general discredited traditional social hierarchies and rules of deference. At the same time, social thought increasingly stressed individual self-interest over collective responsibility, respect for privacy over communality, and a sharp gender division of labor based on male breadwinning and female homemaking—all values and attitudes required for successful employment in the market economy.[4] These transformations left the middle class less sure of how to carry out its self-assigned task of imposing standards of personal behavior on the "lower orders." Middle-class social observers became increasingly suspicious of any departure from the new social expectations and critical of the home life of the poor, which they saw as failing to teach moral rectitude and habits of hard work. "Of all the modes of providing for the poor," declared Boston's Mayor Josiah Quincy in the early 1820s, "the most wasteful, the most expensive and the most injurious to their morals and the industrious habits is that of supply in their own families."[5]

The poor law reforms of 1824 therefore were intended to encourage work on the one hand, and remove the poor from their sin-breeding homes on the other. The local authorities began to ban begging, which was how many of the most indigent had been able to survive, and to replace "outdoor" or "home" relief with workhouses and poorhouses, or "indoor" relief (so-named because the poor had to enter institutions in order to receive aid). Arguing that boarding paupers with private families indulged laziness and eroded the deference that should govern class relations, officials refused outdoor relief to any but the "deserving" poor-defined as those who were not married or not working through no fault of their own. They removed the "undeserving" poor from their homes and placed them in institutions that would teach them proper values and insulate them from the temptations of alcohol, gambling, and idleness. One reformer summed up the new policy: "these characters" had to be placed in almshouses where "prohibiting alcohol and mandating work would stimulate their industry and moral feelings."[6]

During the first half of the nineteenth century, therefore, institutionalization became the preferred method of providing for the poor, efforts being strongest in the New England, mid-Atlantic, and mid-western states. As early as 1820, 80 percent of the relief recipients in thirty-one Pennsylvania counties lived in a poorhouse or a workhouse. In New York, the number of almshouses grew from thirty in 1824 to fifty-five in 1857, while the number of inmates soared from 4,500 in 1830 to 10,000 in 1850. Massachusetts, which had 83 such institutions in 1824, had 219 by 1860.[7] The almshouse rapidly deteriorated into a degraded institution that housed the poor alongside criminals, the physically ill, and the insane. Not surprisingly, all but the most desperate were willing to work for any wage or get married to avoid ending up in these institutions. Although the undifferentiated almshouse gradually gave way to hospitals, prisons, orphanages, reformatories, and mental asylums, within fifty years these separate institutions had also deteriorated into little more than custodial warehouses for the poor-many of whom were by this point foreign born.

New explanations of poverty helped justify the shift from outdoor to indoor relief. Early American society had tolerated poverty, which it understood as God's will: the poor deserved the community's help because they could do little to change their station in life and because aiding them in their own or a neighbor's home, or contracting them out to help work the land, seemed both humane and functional. Industrialization challenged this notion: the country's seemingly unlimited natural resources and its sense of great possibility led to the belief that no one who tried hard need be poor, while the new doctrine of individual responsibility held people responsible for their own personal salvation and economic condition. As the growing relief rolls drained the public treasury, critics began to blame poverty on weak moral character; on the taverns, gambling halls, brothels, and other institutions of the new environment that they believed lured the poor into depraved activities; and on the poor laws themselves.

A second attack on relief began in the 1870s, at a time when rapid economic growth was once again creating a set of social problems. Not only did the post-Civil War boom unleash vast amounts of wealth, but the huge influx of immigrants (16 million of the 20 million people who migrated to the United States in the nineteenth century came after 1860) compounded economic inequality because so many of them were poor. Major depressions in the 1870s, 1880s, and 1890s made the situation worse.

The downturn of 1873-1878, sparked by the collapse of the financial and credit markets, put 3 million people out of work and added many people to the relief rolls. To soothe public fears about the rising cost of public aid, the influential New York Association for the Improvement of the Conditions of the Poor (AICP) condemned the poor for shunning work at lowered wages. The AICP also denounced cash aid, free lunches, and public dormitories for catering to "multitudes of the lower and lowest grades of the poor" and "attracting large numbers of tramps and vagrants to the city."[8] The growing hostility to the poor led New York City to suspend outdoor relief between July 1874 and January 1875,[9] leaving 60,000 people without benefits. New York state cut its outdoor relief costs from $976,600 in 1870 to $749,267 in 1880, despite population growth.[10] Boston reduced spending on outdoor public aid from over $80,300 in 1877 to $64,500 in 1900, while Buffalo lowered its expenses from $73,200 in 1875 to $29,300 in 1880. Philadelphia, Baltimore, San Francisco, and St. Louis, among other cities, followed suit. Many women were affected. Although there is little data on the gender distribution of the poor at that time, in 1875 women made up 40 percent of the 11,000 outdoor relief recipients in Philadelphia; 12.5 percent were men and the rest children under age sixteen.[11]

THE AMERICAN EMIGRANT CAR.

An anti-immigration cartoon from 1882. This catalog of stereotypes includes the Irish with pug noses and wide faces, the Jew with his hook nose and black beard, and, at the center of all the "ruckus," the poor woman with too many babies. [Culver Pictures]

The urban relief rolls also rose during the equally serious downturn of 1882–1885. As in earlier depressions, frantic civic leaders and private charity workers blamed the problem on slipshod relief programs, corrupt politicians, and "ignorant and vicious poor." They also continued to denounce immigration. By 1899, ten of the nation's forty largest cities—home to large numbers of the foreign born—no longer gave outdoor relief, and three others provided very little.[12] As one New York City official put it, it was "better that a few should test the minimum rate [wage] at which existence can be preserved than that the many should find the poorhouse so comfortable a home that they would brave the shame of pauperism to gain admission to it."[13]

Closing relief offices protected the city coffers. It also forced recipients—65 to 75 percent of whom were semi- or unskilled workers—into the labor pool, which helped employers who wanted to replace skilled with unskilled and native-born with foreign-born workers.[14] Industrialists hoped that wage cuts, a longer work day, and the standardization of the labor process through the introduction of machines, supervisors, and simplified work tasks would, together with the greater employment of unskilled labor, increase profits and provide them with greater control of the shop floor.[15] If the pre-Civil War attack on the poor laws had helped to transform a heterogeneous population of farmers and artisans into a waged labor force, the post-Civil War reforms helped employers deskill the workforce and secure greater power over its labor.

As workers found that they were not sharing in the enormous profits that were accruing to business and industry, a labor movement began to gain strength and fight for a greater piece of the economic pie. Unions increased their membership fourfold between 1880 and 1890, created large federations (such as the International Labor Union and the Knights of Labor), and struck for better wages and working conditions in most of the major industries, including steel, mining, and railroads. Industry, which had formed legal trusts, holding companies, and monopolies in order to consolidate its economic power, fought unionization, hired African Americans and immigrants as scabs, and asked the government to call out the militia to put down strikes. Workers also formed political parties, whose demands ranged from the right to work to the redistribution of the nation's wealth. This upsurge of labor activity fueled attacks on public aid that provided workers with an economic back-up. However small, this assistance which enabled workers to avoid the worst jobs also helped them during strikes and anti-union drives.

Beginning in the early 1870s, newly freed black slaves also lost what little government support was available to them. In 1872, pressure from southern landowners who depended on black share-croppers led Congress to close down the federally run Freedman's Bureau, which had been created in 1865 to help several million former slaves gain access to education, training, healthcare, and land. In 1877, Congress abandoned all remaining efforts to break down legal inequality in the South, in effect setting in place the marginalization of African-American labor. In 1883, the Supreme Court voided the 1875 Civil Rights Act, ruling that the Fourteenth Amendment did not prohibit discrimination by and against individuals. Many states then quickly passed Jim Crow segregation laws.

The post-Civil War attack on outdoor relief also targeted those who failed to meet the standards of "proper" family life. This time, belief that poor parents were incapable of socializing their children to fit into industrial society and the pressure to break up poor families was reinforced by new explanations of poverty. Social Darwinism and eugenics claimed that wealth was evidence of fitness while destitution signaled inferiority, that behavior patterns could be inherited, and that relief therefore allowed the "unfit" to propagate and survive. The large number of immigrants fueled the eugenics movement, which also equated the unfit with those who were poor, foreign born, and non-white.

Failure to follow middle-class norms thus became a mark of incompetence. Measured against the white, native-born family ideal, the daily features of poor, immigrant, and working-class life—teeming streets, ramshackle tenements without bathtubs, and crowds of children on the stoops—became "evidence" of parental neglect, family disintegration, and a pervasive "pathology." A New York City charity worker described the homes of the poor as "nurseries of indolence, debauchers, and intemperance," and their inhabitants the "moral pests of society."[16] Instead of recognizing these conditions as expected outcomes of life in overcrowded, impoverished communities, they became the antithesis of the proper home and the root of all social evil.

Middle-class reformers were determined to remove poor children from their families. In 1881, for instance, Charles Hoyt, the secretary of the New York State Board of Charities, recommended that parents in need of relief be prepared to cede their natural rights to the state in order "to break the line of pauper descent."[17] The reformers moved poor immigrant children into "American" homes in order to expose them to "truer" and "finer" family culture and to promote assimilation.[18]

The more that mothers were expected to inculcate proper behavior and social norms, the more women were blamed when things went wrong. Poor law officials often removed a child from his or her home because they believed the mother was inadequate to the task of social control. A "deserving widow" might be allowed to keep one or two of her children, but deserted wives, who were often suspected of colluding with their spouses to get aid, were treated more harshly. Officials reserved the severest response for unmarried mothers, however, and they were often forced to enter the workhouse in order to obtain relief.

The policy of breaking up families reached a peak in the last quarter of the nineteenth century, when the mere prospect of disruptiveness was used to justify removing poor children from their homes. Indeed, the line between protecting a family and disciplining it became hopelessly blurred. Not surprisingly, the number of children placed in orphanages skyrocketed, not only because of court mandates but because many parents had no choice but to place their children in institutions if they were to save them from starvation. By the end of the century, the relief rolls had been reduced, but poverty had also deepened.

CREATING A PROGRAM FOR SINGLE MOTHERS

BY THE EARLY 1900s, 5.3 MILLION WOMEN, OR 20 PERCENT of all women, were working for wages outside the home.[19] Some reformers feared that women took jobs away from men and that their working challenged gender norms-even though most occupations remained sex-segregated. They also worried about the large number of children warehoused in orphanages because their single

A "White Plague" (tuberculosis) poster being shown to Italians in their home, 1908.
[Photo by Byron, from the Byron Collection, Museum of the City of New York]

mothers could not support them or because women worked long hours and had no other source of childcare. And finally, the reformers feared that when poverty forced single mothers to work outside the home, the children who were left unsupervised might become delinquent, and would in any case not be properly prepared for "citizenship." The future of the nation, they argued, depended on proper upbringing by quality mothers in the home. It was these considerations that led to the campaign for Mothers' Pensions, which became the forerunner of AFDC.

The idea of Mothers' Pensions arose during the Progressive Era (1896–1914), a time when both middle-class reformers and the heads of some of the largest corporations wanted more government management of the increasingly complex and volatile economy. Spearheaded by women, the campaign for Mothers' Pensions sought greater government responsibility for the well-being of all poor women and children, but especially widows, who in 1900 headed 77 percent of all mother-only families.[20] Another 16 percent were headed by deserted wives, very few of whom got legal divorces. Unmarried motherhood, rare but on the rise, was more common in black than white households. To avoid public reproach, both deserted wives and single mothers often called themselves widows.

The advocates of Mothers' Pensions therefore focussed on widows and billed the pension as a grant for the special services which these mothers provided and which were necessary for the welfare of the children and the community. By singling out widows, they were able to defang the criticism of those who condemned aid to "immoral" women, and they emphasized that the pension was a payment for the services of motherhood in order to avoid the stigma attached to the traditional "dole." Not surprisingly, then, the "worthy" mothers were more likely to be not only widowed but native-born and white.

However, even "deserving" widows—referred to as "gilt-edged" by some commentators—did not totally escape censure. In exchange for economic support, public officials subjected them to restrictions intended to make sure they conformed to prescribed gender and cultural norms. Agency investigators monitored the women closely for signs of drinking, lax spending, unkempt homes, improper childrearing practices, and relationships with men. They urged foreign-born women to take English and civics classes, cook American dishes, and otherwise conform to white middle-class ways. Middle-class reformers generally accepted the view that immigrants were socially inferior to Anglo Saxons and that poverty was an index of cultural inferiority, although they rejected the biological determinism of nativists and racists. They believed that racial and cultural differences could be transcended and made Mothers' Pensions their instrument for assimilation.

Between 1911 and 1921, forty states enacted Mothers' Pensions, and by 1932 the program existed in all but two states (but not in every county). The pension improved the lives of many poor women and children, but because it stigmatized poor women and welfare, in the long run it opened both to attack. The glorification of Anglo-American motherhood, the belief in childrearing as exclusively women's work, the narrow vision of proper single mothers as widows, and the identification of worthiness with assimilation condemned other mothers who did not live up to these ideals as immoral and unworthy of aid.

Mothers' Pensions also perpetuated the poor law, or charity, model of public assistance: low benefits, sporadic implementation, and emphasis on moral reform. While quieting opposition from private charities that feared competition from public programs and from local officials who worried about state control, these features limited the value of Mothers' Pensions for poor women. The alternatives that were rejected at the time—programs that would serve all children, all poor women as compensation for their caretaking work, and both single and two-parent families (through a family allowance)—assumed that public aid was a right rather than a privilege. Many proponents of these broader programs nevertheless supported Mothers' Pensions, hoping that they would open the door to a larger future role for the government. Had any of the alternatives been accepted, however, programs serving poor families would most likely have been considerably less vulnerable to attack.

THE SOCIAL SECURITY ACT: FROM MOTHERS' PENSIONS TO ADC

THE MOTHERS' PENSION PROGRAM AND ITS PHILOSOPHY of moral reform were incorporated into the 1935 Social Security Act as Aid to Dependent Children (ADC). While the landmark Social Security Act modernized the social welfare system by, among other things, transferring responsibility for social welfare from the states to the federal government, the gender politics of the period meant that the treatment of women, and particularly of unmarried mothers, remained steadfastly traditional.[21]

The mostly male architects of the Social Security Act hoped to insure white, male industrial workers against labor market risks through such measures as unemployment compensation and social security retirement benefits. They displayed little interest in the needs of women, other than as wives of workers. At the same time, the women reformers—the only people with influence in social security circles who were also concerned about poor single women—remained committed to the Mothers' Pension ideal. These women believed that the Mothers' Pension model would serve single mothers better than the employment-based Social Security schemes favored by the planners of the Act. Few in either group believed that Mothers' Pensions would be a source of independence for women.

Officially known as Title IV of the 1935 Social Security Act, Aid to Dependent Children honored motherhood in principle but regulated mothers in practice, and was quite limited in a number of ways. First, Congress rejected a definition of "dependent children" that would have entitled any poor child to assistance as long as the family breadwinner could not work or provide a reasonable subsistence. This interpretation would have allowed the government to aid children living with single parents and children in two-parent homes with unemployed and underemployed fathers, as well as children who were staying with relatives or living in foster homes. In sharp contrast, due in part to strong pressure from employers of cheap labor, especially in the South, who wanted to maintain existing patterns of economic exploitation and racial domination, the final legislation offered assistance only to children deprived of parental support due to the death, continued absence, or incapacity of the family breadwinner.

In addition to limiting ADC to single mothers, Congress rejected proposals to make its benefits compatible with "decency and health." Instead, the grant was capped at $18 per month for the first child and $12 for each additional child. No money was included for a child's caretaker (this did not change until 1950). In contrast, the same legislation provided a maximum of $30 a month for adults receiving Old Age Assistance (OAA) and Aid to the Blind (AB), even though these recipients were not as likely to have children in the home. ADC rules not only forced many mothers into the labor force, but required applicants to pass a demeaning means test to "prove" their lack of income and resources. Congress eventually added this income test to all the public assistance programs. In addition, although the states could set their own benefit levels, few reached the recommended federal maximum. The southern states rationalized their lower-than-average grants by declaring that black families needed less than white families did.

There was also less federal reimbursement for ADC than for the other public assistance programs. Congress provided $1 for every dollar spent by the states on the aged and blind, but only $1 for every $2 spent on dependent children. In 1936, federal expenditures accounted for 43 percent of the Old Age Assistance program, 22 percent of the Aid to the Blind program, and 13 percent of the ADC program. Not surprisingly, state implementation of ADC lagged far behind that of the other programs—so that by the end of 1936, OAA existed in forty-two states and ADC in only twenty-six. By 1940, two-thirds of all eligible children remained uncovered—despite the fact that the ADC caseload had doubled since 1936.

The ADC program perpetuated the Mothers' Pension practice of using public aid to enforce behavioral standards. Both programs categorized women as "deserving" and "undeserving" based on their compliance with traditional marital and family arrangements. But although *all* the Social Security Act programs penalized husbandless women (other than widows), the ADC methods were especially harsh. Shortly after the act's passage and in the name of raising the standards of family life, the Social Security Board called for home visits and periodic eligibility checks. It encouraged the states to make aid contingent on the maintenance of a "suitable" home, which was defined in terms of the mother's sexual, child-bearing, and parenting behavior. Signs of a male presence or the birth of an "illegitimate" child could disqualify a family—making ADC the only public assistance program to impose a morals test on its applicants.

Despite its severe limitations, the ADC program did improve public aid for poor single mothers. First, making ADC and the other public assistance programs federal-state partnerships enlarged federal responsibility for social welfare. Although the states were allowed to set their own eligibility rules and benefit levels, federal oversight led to some national standards and limits on the discretionary power and discriminatory practices of local welfare offices. Perhaps most important, the guarantee of federal matching funds created an entitlement to public aid.

Congress amended the Social Security Act in 1939. The amendments were designed to make Old Age Insurance (OAI) stronger than the public assistance program serving the aged poor (Old Age Assistance, or OAA) by moving up its starting date and by adding special benefits for a deceased worker's surviving dependent widow and children (whether or not the wife herself worked for wages).[22] The transfer of widows from ADC to Social Security further institutionalized ADC as a program just for "undeserving" poor women. For one, the shift further hardened distinctions among women based on marital status. And second, left to serve only the socially unacceptable divorced, separated, and never-married single mothers, ADC grew increasingly stigmatized. The amendments also deepened the act's racial divide: since many black men did not qualify for social security benefits at all, their widows and children could not receive OAI (which was twice what children received on ADC); needy women of color thus had no choice but to apply for assistance.[23] At the same time, the transfer of white widows to OAI ensured that in the future nonwidowed and non-white single mothers would become overrepresented on ADC, leaving the program open to hostility from a public that continued to denigrate the poor, women, and people of color.

THE POSTWAR ATTACK, 1945-1960

THE WELFARE STATE EXPANDED RAPIDLY AFTER THE
Second World War , fueled by population growth, postwar prosperity, the liberalization of existing programs, a greater sense of
public responsibility for social problems, the ability of the nation
to meet the needs of the poor more adequately, and demands for
greater economic security from both the trade union and civil
rights movements. During the postwar boom, Congress extended
social insurance coverage to some (but not all) of the farm, domestic, and self-employed workers who had been left out of the original act. It added cash assistance for ADC mothers in 1950 and
benefits for disabled workers in 1956. Congress also enacted a
national School Lunch Program (1946), the Mental Health Act
(1946), the Hill-Burton Hospital Construction Act (1946), the
Employment Act (1946), the Housing Act (1949), the School Milk
Program (1954), and the Vocational Rehabilitation Act (1954).
This growing social welfare system was designed to protect the
unprotected against what were increasingly seen as the uncontrollable risks faced by individuals and families living and working in
an industrial society. They also benefitted many middle-class families and not a few corporations, which depended on these programs to ensure consumer buying power, to keep the workforce
healthy and educated, and in general to maintain the social peace.

The expansion and liberalization of the welfare state during
the late 1940s and early 1950s did not go uncontested. While
advocates continued to press for improvements, opponents in and
outside of the Republican Congress argued that the welfare state
represented "big government" and "creeping socialism." Fueled by
postwar anti-communism and rising conservatism, ADC in particular was attacked by the Eisenhower administration and by many
governors, even though it was not by any means the largest or
most expensive welfare program. The hostility was fueled by regular press reports proclaiming that the ADC rolls had risen from
372,000 in 1940 to 803,000 in 1960, while spending had jumped

from $130 million in 1940 to $550 million in 1950 to $995 million in 1960.[24] However, the press failed to note that during these twenty years the number of women on welfare fluctuated with changes in social and economic conditions. Between 1936 and 1940, the Depression and ADC's start-up enrollments raised the rolls from 162,000 to 372,000 families. The numbers fell during World War II, due to the increased demand for female labor. Between 1945 and 1950, wages and salaries rose 23 percent, but inflation and unemployment also took a toll, so that in 1950 one-fifth of the population lived in poverty.[25] Prices continued to rise even during the first postwar economic slump, which began in 1949, and unemployment grew steadily, abating only when the Korean war provided a brief economic stimulus. Welfare rolls declined during the war but increased again during the recessions of 1953–1954 and 1957–1958. By 1960, 20 percent of all whites, nearly 50 percent of people living in female-headed households, and more than half of all African Americans were poor, so the rolls began to rise again.[26]

The attack on welfare was fueled by anxieties about public spending that arose when the government introduced a payroll deduction system that transformed the income tax from a class tax (a tax on the top income groups) to a mass tax (one that affected nearly all workers). By 1943, 40 million people from all social classes were paying federal income taxes, up from only 4 million (mostly affluent) people in 1939.[27] This happened at the same time that more was being spent on ADC. As a result, by the 1950s the white middle class was more than ready to scapegoat those receiving public aid.

Ignoring the clear link between lower wages, fewer jobs, economic recession, and the increased number of women applying for ADC, politicians and the media attacked the program. From the early 1940s to the 1960s, critics cut benefits, stiffened eligibility rules, investigated local welfare departments for fraud, and otherwise tried to keep women off the rolls. As in earlier periods, they blamed the expansion of ADC not on the economy but on the behavior of poor women and the availability of relief. As a New York City domestic relations court judge told reporters, "The relief set up is sapping the will to work, encouraging cynicism and petty chiseling." The popular news magazines revived negative stereotypes of welfare mothers as "lazy" and "immoral," and painted lurid pictures of welfare recipients as women who spent money on maids, TV sets, cars, and jewelry. The headline of one popular mass-circulation magazine declared: "Want $3680 a year, tax free? You are required only to have no self-respect and never get a job. Buy all the liquor you want . . . and the welfare department will help you."[28]

Welfare, Women's Work, and the Labor Market

The anti-welfare rhetoric masked one of the underlying reasons for the attack on ADC: the competing demand for women's unpaid labor in the home and their low-paid labor in the market. This chronic tension intensified during the postwar years because the occupations that relied heavily on female workers were expanding while demographic shifts and postwar attitudes toward women's work were shrinking the pool of women who might have filled these jobs.

To begin with, the female labor force was not growing fast enough to meet the demand. The number of women who typically worked outside the home—older, widowed, and divorced women—remained stable, while low prewar birth rates and high postwar marriage rates reduced the supply of young single women available for work. Since older married white women with grown children were already working in large numbers, they could not fill the gap. Racism made employers reluctant to hire African-American women, who had always worked outside the home, in these new and better jobs.

The growing demand for women workers also conflicted with widespread fears that there would not be enough jobs for the returning soldiers. While ending war-related production freed several hundred thousand women up for other jobs,[29] many of them withdrew from the labor force because of the strains of combining housekeeping with paid employment and in response to the post-war campaign to send women back into the home. The mass media told women it was their patriotic duty to give up their jobs to returning soldiers, maligned employed women as unfeminine "Amazons" who could outdrink, outswear, and outswagger men, and popularized social science research which proclaimed that working wives created marital friction, family instability, and neurotic children.[30] By 1950 there was a net drop in the rate at which married mothers aged twenty-five to thirty-four with young children were going to work.[31] The Women's Bureau, by 1953, was reporting severe shortages of typists, stenographers, nurses, teachers, social workers, and medical aides.[32] The GI Bill exacerbated overall labor shortages by enabling millions of returning veterans to attend college instead of entering the labor market.

Working-class women who could not afford to stay home met some of the demand, but rather than keeping their higher paying wartime jobs in industry, they were bumped into lower paying "women's" jobs. The demand for women workers eventually helped black women to win higher wages in domestic work, or even to avoid it altogether, but this in turn created panic among white middle-class housewives, and lead the Women's Bureau to develop programs to train black women for service. By 1950, 60 percent of black women, but only 16 percent of white women, worked in private households or institutional service jobs.[33]

African Americans who were dislocated by the mechanization of southern agriculture and women on welfare were two additional sources of labor. In the late 1940s and 1950s, many states forced women to work by lowering ADC benefits and restricting access to the program.[34] Officials publicized the names of recipients to deter people from seeking aid. To weed out suspected "frauds" and to otherwise harass recipients, some welfare departments closed out entire caseloads and then required everyone to reapply, hoping that many would not want to undergo another eligibility investigation. In the early 1950s, after the Eisenhower administration pressed for greater local control of welfare, state after state added punitive administrative policies in order to remove recipients from the rolls and slow new applications. In states that did not actively deny women benefits or require that they work part-time, welfare departments made sure that those receiving aid were less well-off than those who were working by subtracting one ADC dollar for every dollar earned.

The effort to enlarge the labor pool by restricting welfare was especially intense in the South.[35] From the days of slavery, white society had valued African-American women as workers and denied them the protection and rights of womanhood granted to white women. During the 1940s and 1950s, southern states intentionally restricted welfare in order to force black women to work. In 1943, Louisiana refused aid to mothers with young children who appeared "employable," especially during the harvest season. In 1952, Georgia directed local welfare boards to deny all applications (and close all cases) of employable mothers in "periods of full employment," that is, when they were needed in the cotton and tobacco fields; a similar "farm policy" was adopted in Arkansas in 1953. In 1954, a Louisiana civic leader explicitly complained that "public assistance results in reducing the unskilled labor . . . in employment where women and children form a principal part of the supply." Southern employers believed there was "no reason why the employable Negro mother should not continue her usually sketchy seasonal labor or indefinite domestic service rather than receive a public assistance grant," and many local welfare departments gave black women less money than they did to white women. In addition, the strict enforcement of year-long state residency requirements prevented many African-American women (as well as southwestern Latina migrants) from receiving aid. A nationwide study conducted by the Department of Health, Education, and Welfare in 1961 reported that 19 percent of black mothers on welfare worked, compared to only 10 percent of white mothers on welfare, and most of those who were working lived in the South.[36]

Forcing women on welfare to work not only helped fill jobs at the bottom rungs of the employment ladder in the expanding service sector, but also reproduced and enforced patterns of racial domination during a period of growing racial tension and militant protest. The increased competition between blacks and whites for jobs and housing contributed to a wave of anti-black violence in 1944, including major conflagrations in Detroit, Michigan; Harlem, New York; Mobile, Alabama; and Beaumont, Texas. Black workers won a ban against discrimination in defense production (1941), the elimination of the all-white primary (1944), and presidential support for desegregating the military (1948). In the mid-1950s, emboldened by the 1954 Supreme Court ban on separate-but-equal schools, the civil rights movement shed its original "go slow" strategy and launched an all-out attack on segregation. In 1955, blacks organized the Montgomery Bus Boycott. In August 1957, Congress passed the first Civil Rights Act in eighty-two years; in September the President sent troops to Arkansas so that black students could enter Central High School. As we will see in Part 4, southern black women formed the backbone of the ensuing boycotts, mass demonstrations, civil disobedience, and voter registration drives. Blacks, including women, had become "uppity" and had to be put in their place.

Women, Welfare, and the Family

In their effort to reduce the rolls, the postwar welfare critics also targeted poor women's marital and childbearing patterns. The rising demand for women workers challenged women's traditional relationship to the family by reducing their economic dependence on men. So did the "epidemic" of marital break-ups and out-of-wedlock births which resulted from hasty wartime unions, the stress of wartime separations, as well as greater self-reliance on the part of women who had lived alone and/or earned their own incomes during the war. The divorce rate climbed from 16 per 100 marriages in 1940 to 25 per 100 in 1950 (more, if separations are included). Nonmarital births among women aged fifteen to forty-four tripled between 1940 and 1960, rising from 7.1 to 21.6 per 1,000 women. The rate for white women jumped from 3.6 to 9.2 per 1,000; the rate for black women, which was already much higher, increased somewhat more slowly, from 35.6 to 98.3 per 1,000.[37]

The high rates of marital break-ups and non-marital births among blacks stemmed in part from wartime dislocations, but also from persistent black male unemployment and the strains of both racism and poverty. On the other hand, the black community showed a greater willingness to sustain women on their own, to respect women's employment, and to share child raising among extended networks of kin.[38]

The changes in family structure among women in all walks of life heightened concerns about what we today call "family values" and led to a panic about the breakdown of the family and the "proper" role for women. This in turn fueled the attack on ADC. Social scientists, policymakers, and mental health professionals raised questions about the ability of working women to raise children and blamed truancy, running away, juvenile delinquency, and almost every other personal and social problem on mothers—underinvolved or overinvolved white mothers and overbearing or emasculating black matriarchs. Public concern about these issues was projected onto poor women and the ADC program. The experts reported that poor "hard-to-reach" families-many headed by women-were the breeding ground for social problems and absorbed most of the social welfare resources.[39] The criticism of single mothers extended to the ADC program which, reflecting both the transfer of widows to the Social Security program and changing family patterns in wider society, now served many fewer widows and many more divorced, separated, and never-married women, all of whom were still considered immoral and undeserving of aid.[40]

The assault on ADC was compounded by the dramatic postwar change in the racial composition of the welfare rolls. Before World War II, black women comprised between 14 and 17 percent of all women on ADC—a number that would have been higher if welfare departments had not discriminated against them. After the war, the black portion of the ADC caseload grew rapidly, from 21 percent in 1942 to 30 percent in 1948 to 48 percent in 1961.[41] As this occurred, the animosity surrounding public assistance shifted its focus from immigrants to blacks, and the justification for cutting aid changed from preserving the "purity of the native stock" to evoking racial stereotypes of black women as promiscuous, matriarchal, and welfare-dependent. The racial tensions were apparent in newspaper headlines: "It Pays to Play the Pauper," read one headline in *Nation's Business* in 1950. Another proclaimed that "Relief Is Ruining Families." A 1961 article in *Look* magazine, entitled "Welfare: Has It Become Scandal?" complained that relief . . . had spawned a vicious cycle in welfare so that now a second generation is maturing on the welfare rolls. The girls [in these families] take their pregnancies as a matter of course. The home is like Grand Central Terminal. . . . All the girls should have been put in homes.[42]

The federal and state governments responded to this public barrage by penalizing women for their marital and childbearing choices.[43] Much of the anti-welfare activity took the form of "substitute father" and "man-in-the-house" rules designed to force men into paying child support, to prevent them from living off a women's welfare check, and to enforce sexual norms. Some states penalized a woman for having a relationship with a man who did not have a blood relationship to her children. In 1950, for instance, South Carolina concluded that children were not "deprived" of parental support if there was "any man with whom the mother had a common-law relationship, even if he did not stay in the home regularly or support the children." Alabama reduced its rolls by 25 percent by cutting women who were "going with a man," Arkansas denied aid to mothers engaged in a "non-stable, non-legal union," Michigan to families with male "borders," and Texas to "pseudo-common law" marriages. To enforce these regulations, welfare investigators pried into the private lives of recipients, in many cases conducting midnight raids to catch men visiting overnight in welfare homes.

By 1950 more than half the states had also passed "suitable home" laws that limited aid to "fit" mothers.[44] In 1951, the governor of Georgia declared that he was "willing to tolerate an unwed mother who makes one mistake, but not when the mistake is repeated three, four, or five times." His welfare department denied aid to children born to unwed women on the rolls. In 1960, as part of a package "to counteract racial integration," Louisiana made it a crime to have more than one "illegitimate" child and struck more than 20,000 children from the program. In 1961, Newburgh, New York, imposed time limits on ADC, removed children from "unsuitable homes," and cut the benefits for unwed ADC mothers who had additional children while receiving aid. North Carolina officials went even as far as discussing the sterilization of ADC women to reduce their costs!

THE WELFARE CRISIS AND WELFARE REFORM, 1967-1972

THE SECOND MAJOR ATTACK ON WELFARE IN THE twentieth century took place at the end of the 1960s. The welfare rolls had grown dramatically during this decade (and especially after 1964), particularly in urban centers in the North and the West. The number of families receiving ADC rose from 803,000 in 1960 to about 1 million in 1965 and then shot up to 1.9 million in 1970 and to just under 3 million in 1972. Benefit payments increased from $995 million in 1960 to $7 billion in 1972. Moreover, the numbers climbed steadily even when conditions improved—during the Vietnam War, for instance—and despite a drop in the poverty rate, from 22 percent of the population in 1960 to 12 percent in 1972.[45]

What the press called the welfare "explosion" was in fact the result of a complex set of social, economic, and political forces. First, the continued growth of the population, of families headed by women, and of poor families swelled the rolls. By 1969, 24 million people lived in poverty, and the wages of many workers were no longer keeping pace with the rising cost of living. The liberalization of welfare policy had also played a role. In 1961, Congress raised the ADC need standard. The 1962 Social Security Act amendments allowed women on welfare to work and collect benefits, permitted the states to provide services to a broad range of current and potential recipients, made a limited group of two-parent households eligible for aid—it was at this point that the name was changed from ADC to Aid to Families with Dependent Children, or AFDC.

Finally, political pressures contributed to the expansion of AFDC. The growing strength of the civil rights movement in the North, the massive March on Washington in 1963, the 1964 and 1968 uprisings by large numbers of marginalized African Americans, and the emergence of the black power movement forced the Democratic Party to support both civil rights and social welfare legislation.[46] The push to reform welfare was furthered by the organization of thousands of welfare mothers into the highly effective National Welfare Rights Union (NWRO) which brought attention to the plight of poor women and fear of more disorder into the hearts of local civic and business leaders (we will return to this period in Part 4).

Since the majority of African Americans in the North lived in a few large cities in states with many electoral votes, politicians began to worry that they had the votes to swing presidential elections. Some blacks had already threatened to bolt the Democratic Party to protest its sluggish civil rights record. Hoping to hold onto its black constituents, to mute civil rights protests, and to prevent more ghetto uprisings, the liberal wing of the party engineered the passage of the Civil Rights Act (1964), the Voting Rights Act (1965), and Medicaid and Medicare (1965). In 1964, the Democrats also launched a "war on poverty," which promoted the "maximum feasible participation" of the poor in civic affairs and funded city agencies to develop new healthcare, childcare, employment, and legal services. Congress extended AFDC to children between the ages of eighteen and twenty-one who were still attending school

(1964) and to children in foster care (1969), and raised the standard of need (1969). By 1970, the Supreme Court had invalidated restrictive residency requirements, the intrusive "man-in-the-house" rules, and the onerous "substitute-father" regulations.

Not surprisingly, the proportion of applicants accepted for AFDC jumped, from 62 percent in 1965 to 74 percent in 1969. And once state barriers dropped, the program served even more unmarried women, while the proportion of blacks rose slightly, from 46 in 1961 to a peak of 49 percent in 1967. The value of welfare benefits increased by 36 percent from 1965 to 1970, compared to a 27 percent increase from 1955 to 1960 and a 19 percent increase from 1950 to 1955. Since only half of all eligible women actually applied for AFDC, experts fearfully predicted that the rolls would rise even farther and that federal AFDC costs would increase, possibly reaching $1.84 billion by 1972.[47] By the late 1960s, many politicians and social analysts were arguing that the program had become too large and costly and needed to be "reformed."

As in the past, two underlying issues loomed large in the ensuing attack: the relationship between welfare and the labor market, and the relationship between welfare and family life. But the particulars that sparked the attack were different: this time, instead of labor shortages, the main problem was that welfare benefits had begun to exceed wages. In addition, never-married, rather than previously married, women were increasingly appearing on the rolls.

Low Wages and Labor Shortages

In the late 1960s, welfare critics began to argue that AFDC had become more attractive than work. For instance, in his 1967 inaugural address as governor of California, Ronald Reagan declared, "We are not going to perpetuate poverty by substituting a permanent dole for a paycheck. There is no humanity in destroying self-reliance, dignity and self-respect—the very substance of moral fiber." Wilbur Mills, chair of the House Ways and Means Committee, asked, "Is it in the public interest for welfare to become a way of life?" In late 1965, a Chicago cab driver expressed a widespread point of view: "The goddamn people sit around when they should be working and they're having illegitimate kids to get more money. You know their morals are different. They don't give a damn."[48]

The pressure to retrench welfare reflected more than growing costs or a backlash against nonwhite recipients, however. It also reflected a feeling that AFDC no longer regulated the workforce effectively. A change in the relationship between wages and welfare benefits in high-benefit states made AFDC more economically attractive than full-time work, and this in turn made it harder for AFDC rules to force women into the labor force when needed. Between 1947 and 1962, both ADC payments and wages rose by two-thirds, but because they rose in tandem, the smaller ADC grant remained below the market wage. In sharp contrast, between 1960 and 1970, the average earnings of workers rose by 48 percent, while the average AFDC benefits jumped 75 percent. In the early 1970s, the AFDC grant exceeded the minimum wage in many high-benefit states.[49] Even though it did this by only a small amount, welfare became an economically rational choice for some poor women.

This shift in the relationship between welfare and wages violated a fundamental rule of public assistance: that its benefits remain below the lowest prevailing wage to ensure that only the most desperate will choose it over work. The shift also made it harder to move AFDC mothers in and out of the workforce on an as-needed basis, much less to channel them permanently into the labor market. Economists and politicians blamed the rising rolls on "high" benefits instead of low wages and worried that, if left unchanged, AFDC would erode the work ethic, reduce the labor supply, and, in the prevailing tight labor market, force wages up. Rather than raise wages for all women, the experts decided to make work a requirement for receiving AFDC.

Until this time, federal AFDC rules had prohibited women on welfare from working; this had been enforced by charging any casual earnings against the relief grant (so a women who combined welfare and part-time work would not be better off than a women working for wages full time). As described above, many states tried to sidestep these procedures, and when the federal government clamped down, they found other ways to limit access: Arizona passed a closed-end appropriation to reduce funding if the AFDC program grew bigger than the budget; Connecticut instituted a flat-grant system that eliminated payment for special needs; Kansas cut AFDC benefits 20 percent across the board; Maine eliminated AFDC for unemployed fathers (AFDC-UP); New Jersey replaced AFDC-UP with assistance to the working poor that paid two-thirds of the AFDC standard; Nebraska cut payments 10 percent; Texas cut its maximum payment for a family from $135 to $125 a month—and so on.

In 1962, Congress also attempted to get welfare mothers to work by using such incentives as training and social services to increase their employability. But this "rehabilitation" or "social service" strategy did not reduce the welfare rolls quickly enough. Instead of waiting for longer term outcomes, impatient legislators, led by Wilbur Mills, cracked down and included a tough work program, called the Work Incentive Program (WIN) as part of the 1967 amendments to the Social Security Act.[50] WIN required women on welfare to find work or to register for some kind of employment and training program. Although mothers receiving AFDC could keep part of their earnings while receiving the full welfare grant, WIN was nevertheless coercive: for the first time in the history of the program, any mother with children over the age of 6 had to work or participate in a job-training or work program in order to receive a grant. If she refused she risked losing her welfare check. WIN was followed in 1971 by the Talmadge Amendment, or WIN II, which further stiffened work requirements, scuttled WIN's job-training programs, and strengthened sanctions for noncompliance, including penalties for states that failed to enroll enough recipients into the program.

WIN II's budget grew to more than $300 million in 1974 (where it remained until 1981, when it began to decline), but enrollment fell below expectations. For one, welfare department staff could not handle all the new registrants. Moreover, federal rules exempted sick and disabled women from the work requirements, as well as mothers who were needed at home to care for young children or who had no childcare services available. (It is important to note here that within welfare circles, many still believed that women belonged at home.) The program also ignored the fact that low earnings enabled WIN participants to work and still qualify for some AFDC benefits, and that many AFDC recipients already combined welfare and work. The ambivalence about sending women to work, as well as outright sex discrimination, also led WIN workers to place more welfare fathers (from the small AFDC-UP program) than mothers in the WIN work programs. Whites, who made up less than half of the AFDC caseload, received far more than half of the available job placements.

WIN II remained in place until it was superseded by JOBS, the work program that was part of the 1988 Family Support Act (described in Part 1). Despite its limitations, WIN processed 800,000 recipients a year. While not everyone ended up with a job, the employment of women on welfare increased by 25 percent or more in fifteen states, 50 percent or more in nine states, and over 100 percent in three states. At the same time, WIN's combination of harsh rules and strict work incentives added to the low-wage labor supply by channeling thousands of AFDC mothers into low-paid jobs and by deterring unknown numbers of women from applying for aid in the first place. By increasing the size of the labor pool, WIN also helped to keep wages down, in effect subsidizing low-wage employers, instead of pressing them to make work more attractive than welfare by raising wages.

A Woman's Right to Choose

The attack on welfare in the late 1960s and early 1970s also targeted women's social and sexual autonomy. In the 1960s, large numbers of people became alarmed about relaxed sexual norms (casual sex, easier divorces, increased cohabitation), changing family structures (falling birth rates, later marriages, more middle-class single mothers), and a permissive youth culture (college dropouts, drug use, singles' bars).

The trend toward women and children living on their own was continuing: in the 1960s, one in twenty unmarried women had a child; by 1970, the number had jumped to one in ten. Further, the numbers understated the extent of change since they excluded many pregnant women who married, shotgun or not, before their children were born. The growth of AFDC reflected these wider societal trends,[51] as well as the activities of the National Welfare Rights Organization, the War on Poverty, and the public debate about reforming public assistance, all of which made more single mothers aware of the availability of AFDC. However, instead of acknowledging that the growth of never-married single mothers on AFDC stemmed even in part from these trends, the welfare critics put unwed mothers on AFDC forward as the prime example of a growing danger: the decline in family stability.

In addition, the women's movement made patriarchy and sexism public issues for the first time since the early 1900s. Calls for reproductive freedom, equal employment rights, and the end of male control of women's lives, as well as a spotlight on rape, incest, and battering, awakened large numbers of middle-class women to gender oppression on the job and at home. Welfare provided women with an alternative to such oppression, however limited, and appeared to endorse the idea that women could choose among depending on men (marriage), the labor market, or the state for economic support. Although only poor and working-class women could apply for AFDC, and although many did not actually take up the opportunity, the availability of welfare seemed to permit more female autonomy than the wider society was prepared to grant. To make matters worse, by the end of the decade the patriarchal underpinnings of welfare had also become part of a welfare rights critique. In her path-breaking 1972 article, "Welfare Is a Women's Issue," Johnnie Tillmon, president of the

National Welfare Rights Organization, linked the concerns of poor and middle-class women as follows:

> There are a lot of other lies that male society tells about welfare mothers: that AFDC mothers are immoral, that AFDC mothers are lazy, misuse their welfare checks, spend it all on booze and are stupid and incompetent. If people are willing to believe these lies, it's partly because they are just special versions of the lies that society tells about all women. For instance, the notion that AFDC mothers are lazy: that's just a negative version of the idea that women don't work and don't want to. It's a way of rationalizing the male policy of keeping women as domestic slaves. The notion that AFDC mothers are immoral is another way of saying that all women are likely to become whores unless they're kept under control by men and marriage.[52]

In addition to maligning women on welfare as lazy, the attack on welfare, as Tillmon pointed out, reflected public anxieties about the growing personal and sexual autonomy of women.

Translating fears of female autonomy into concerns about "proper" motherhood, the welfare critics attacked the right of poor women to bear children on their own. In 1966, when Congress modified the Social Security Act to allow the states to move children into foster care if their home environments were poor, "illegitimacy" was chosen as the main indicator of this condition. The 1967 Amendments froze federal funds for AFDC cases that could be attributed to desertion or nonmarital births, but maintained funding for "properly" married women-widowed AFDC mothers and wives in AFDC-UP households. Driven by the unsubstantiated view that women in poverty deliberately have children to increase their welfare grants, these federal rules penalized the states for any increase in the proportion of "illegitimate" children in their AFDC caseloads. Congress never implemented (and eventually repealed) the freeze, but only after two years of pressure from the social service establishment, civil rights organizations, and the welfare rights movement. Nevertheless, the assault continued at the local level. In 1971, a Tennessee legislator introduced a bill to sterilize unwed mothers who applied for welfare on pain of losing custody of their children. In 1972, a California welfare advisory board proposed that any woman who had a third nonmarital child should be declared unfit and be forced to hand the third child over to the state. Similar rules to limit women's right to choose also went into effect in other states.[53]

Black women again took the brunt of the attack. For instance, Julius Horowitz, writing for *New York Times Magazine* in 1965, implied that black single mothers lacked maternal commitment when he wrote, "We know that the damage to the infant takes place long before he [sic] sees the dirt, the drunks, the drug addicts, the spilled garbage of the slum; the damage takes place when the unavailable mother brings her child home from the hospital and realizes she hates him for being alive."[54] Daniel Patrick Moynihan's controversial report, *The Negro Family* (1965), focused on welfare, delinquency, unemployment, drug addiction, and school failure in the black community, concluding that its social problems were unique and stemmed almost exclusively from the "breakdown" of the family.[55] Moynihan ignored both the strengths of the black family and the impact of poverty and racial inequality on its well-being, and overestimated the differences between poor black and poor white families.

STILL MORE WELFARE REFORM

THE ATTACK ON POOR WOMEN AS LAZY AND IMMORAL continued during the 1970s, despite the stabilization of the welfare rolls. Meanwhile, the falling standard of living for two-parent, working-class households began to create problems for both political parties. In 1968, thousands of disaffected white Democrats voted Republican. Desirous of wooing these voters, both parties supported policies that targeted their needs. Nixon's Family Assistance Plan (1971) and Carter's Better Jobs and Income Program

(1976) tried to extend welfare to two-parent families headed by men. Congress defeated these bills, but, to give working families a boost, it legislated new job-creation programs (Public Employment Program, 1971; Comprehensive Employment and Training Program, CETA, 1973) and tax credits (Earned Income Tax Credit, EITC, 1976). By the early 1980s, both parties concurred that the government should do more for the working poor by ensuring that work paid more than welfare, which ignored the interdependence and overlap between the working and the welfare poor. Although he cut CETA, Ronald Reagan raised the deeply eroded minimum wage for the first time in eight years. In 1986, 1990, and 1992 Congress expanded the EITC with strong support from Presidents Reagan, Bush, and Clinton. However, in the increasingly conservative climate of the mid-1990s, even the effort to please the economically anxious "angry white men" gave way to greater interest in protecting military spending, balancing the budget, and extending tax cuts for the rich.

The short-lived effort to use welfare, job creation, and tax credits to improve the lot of working families supported by men contrasts sharply with the historically harsh assaults on poor families headed by women. As a program just for single mothers, welfare once again became a ready target for cuts in the economic recovery plan launched in 1981 by Reagan and followed by Bush and Clinton. As in the past, the assault targeted women's work behavior, family choices, and social programs rather than the underlying causes of poverty. In the late 1990s, having lost the long welfare reform battle, even some advocates for poor women have replaced demands for welfare rights and a guaranteed income for all families with demands for job creation and a living wage. Hopefully, these otherwise important campaigns will include income support programs and a guaranteed income for those who cannot work and recognize the reality that job and wage oriented policies alone have historically failed to redress the inequality faced by women and persons of color.

Although Parts 1 and 2 have focused on the attacks on women and welfare, it would be a mistake to assume that women have taken these attacks lying down. Part 4 will describe their activism in some detail. However, before turning to "the streets," we need to look at the colleges and universities where feminist scholars have fought to reform the prevailing theories of the welfare state so that they might better represent the lives of women.

PART THREE

The Gendered Welfare State

IN LEGISLATURES AND UNIVERSITIES ACROSS THE UNITED States, women have struggled with the issues raised by welfare reform. While welfare mothers and their advocates have agitated for less punitive and more responsive social welfare programs, feminist scholars have had to shoulder their way into debates surrounding the origins and function of the welfare state. Although women predominate among welfare clients and workers, for years the academic community remained strikingly silent on the gender issues that welfare raises. The men who dominated welfare research and policymaking approached the subject by focusing on white male workers and their female dependents. These theorists investigated workplaces, labor markets, trade unions, political parties, and other institutions that have traditionally barred women. Their research findings were generalized to women of all races, and to women and men of color.

While these analyses have made important contributions to our knowledge of the welfare state, they have focussed on the dynamics of labor markets, capitalist economics, and class struggle without paying systematic attention to the dynamics of families, to patriarchal arrangements, and to gender issues. Volumes of research document how the welfare state creates and mediates class inequality, but until feminists came on the scene we knew next to nothing about how it creates and mediates gender inequality. Social welfare may be part of the problem for women, but it could be part of the solution as well. This section reviews the feminist critiques of the liberal, social citizenship, and traditional Marxist theories of the welfare state, describes some of the feminist correctives, and then suggests social welfare policies that might better address the needs of women and men. The analysis draws on liberal, cultural (radical), and socialist feminist thinking because taken together these scholars have shown that gender matters.

GENDER MATTERS

AN EXPLORATION OF THE LONG-STANDING BUT RELATIVELY unstudied relationship between women and the welfare state needs to begin with a review of four distinct but interrelated sources of gender inequality: sexism, patriarchy, the gender division of labor, and social reproduction. These key gender aspects of our social structure are important for the feminist critique presented here because they have shaped most of our societal institutions, including the welfare state. Each of the different feminist approaches emphasizes some of these dimensions more than others: the liberal feminists emphasize sexism, the cultural feminists highlight patriarchy, and the socialist feminists focus on social reproduction and the gender division of labor. However, we need to know about each of these four features of society in order to understand the relationship between women and the welfare state.

Sexism, which is central to the liberal feminist analysis of the welfare state, refers to the belief that a person's ability, intelligence, and character are rooted in biology rather than shaped by external forces; that males naturally possess more of certain desired traits and are therefore superior; and that, due to their alleged "inferiority," women can legitimately be denied equal rights and opportunities. Sexism can appear in both individual and institutional forms. Individual sexism refers to overt attitudes and behavior, from beliefs that prejudge others (i.e., prejudice) to the differential treatment of people based on their group association (i.e., discrimination). Institutional sexism refers to the ways in which laws, policies, or practices systematically create and enforce prevailing sexual inequities. Whether or not the individuals involved have sexist intentions, or are even aware of these outcomes, if institutional processes yield sexist consequences, the institution in question can be considered sexist.

Racism works in much the same way as sexism, benefiting some at the expense of others and thus perpetuating the power of a dominant group. The resulting inequality is then justified by ideologies and theories that assert that the uneven distribution of power, resources, and privileges is biologically based and therefore "natural," inevitable, and difficult to change. By dividing similarly oppressed groups that might otherwise join forces and fight for a bigger share of the proverbial pie, or even for a new and better one, both "isms" camouflage the real power of those who benefit most from keeping others down.

The concept of *patriarchy* is central to cultural feminist analysis of the welfare state.[1] While sexism underscores the unequal treatment of individuals on the basis of their sex, patriarchy speaks to the unequal distribution of power between *all* women and *all* men. Originally defined as the "rule of the father," the term has been broadened to include the structural and ideological arrangements that enable men as a group to dominate women as a group. Patriarchy is thus the institutionalization of male dominance throughout society, and as such diminishes women's control over their choices about childrearing, mothering, laboring, and loving. The distribution of the privileges of patriarchy vary sharply by class and race, so that some men benefit more than others. The strength and manifestations of patriarchal power also shift with changes in the wider social order.

Patriarchy is enforced by the ideology of gender roles. Ideology is the collection of symbols and beliefs that are integrally tied to social and political power. Ideologies are transmitted to members of a society through the language and images of everyday life, in formal institutions, and by the "isms" described above. Like all ideologies, the ideology of gender roles gives meaning to social relations, shapes how people think and act, and upholds prevailing relations of power by (among other things) rewarding conforming behavior and discrediting alternatives—such as mother-only households or lesbian couples—as wrong or even dangerous.

While remaining at the core of much feminist analysis, the concept of patriarchy has evoked considerable debate within feminist ranks. Some feminists have argued that it is difficult to operationalize and that it has embedded in it the notion of women as victims. Others have debated the roots of patriarchy, grounding it alternatively in biology, psychology, culture, social structure, and ideology. Most feminists, however, recognize that patriarchy is central to women's oppression.

The *gender division of labor* is the third source of gender inequality. It is particularly emphasized by socialist feminists, who link male domination to the economic dependence of women on men. Standard social science theories used to hold that the assignment of breadwinning roles to men and homemaking roles to women was not only natural but contributed to the smooth functioning of the family and society. Feminists generally argue that this arrangement is socially constructed—and that it is also patriarchal and oppressive to women.

The modern gender division of labor appeared in the early 1800s, as the Industrial Revolution gradually separated production for the household from production for the market. The developing factory system drew men out of the home. At the same time, family life, once intimately linked to economic activity, became a distinct and specific arena, with women in charge of parenting, homemaking, and caretaking. The shift to a market economy, and the allocation of waged work to men and domestic work to women, eventually devalued women's work in the home (as it was unwaged), and left women economically dependent on men.

A new ideology of gender roles reinforced the emerging division of labor. The social norms of the period, which I call the "family ethic,"[2] equated masculinity with waged labor, male domination, and breadwinning; and femininity with unpaid labor, female subordination, and caretaking. This arrangement was legitimized by the belief that male and female roles were biologically determined; by legal doctrines that defined women as the property of men; and by laws that barred women from the workforce, denied them the right to make contracts or own property, and excluded them from political participation, including the vote. The family ethic defined white middle- and upper-class women as fragile and pure and confined them to the home.

In the years before the Civil War, while the family ethic glorified and "protected" white middle-class women, slavery was brutalizing black women, forcing them to work in the fields and to breed children for masters who routinely tore their families apart.[3] After slavery was abolished, this double standard of womanhood continued: black women were expected to work while white middle-class women were expected to stay home.

The double standard also applied to white working-class women. Although skilled white male workers fought for a "family wage" through their unions and political parties, it was not until the end of the nineteenth century that they earned enough to be the family's sole breadwinner. In the absence of a wage that provided a man with enough income to allow his wife to stay home, raise the children, and maintain the family, many working-class women had to earn an income: young single women went to work in the new mills and factories, while wives either joined them or took in boarders, sewing, or laundry.

The family ethic persisted well into the twentieth century. When challenged by the massive entry of women into the labor force after the Second World War, the family ethic expanded to incorporate women's employment—but the gender roles were maintained because this work was defined as temporary, as secondary to a woman's family duties, and as an exception to the norm. In addition, women were segregated into low-paid "female" jobs and their income was labelled pin money, trousseau money, or the "second" income.

The family ethic has also survived the challenges of rising divorce rates, single motherhood, childless couples, alternative methods of conception, gay and lesbian parenting, the women's movement, and, most recently, the declining standard of living, but not without causing a backlash against women's rights. Today's call for a return to "family values" is part of an effort to restore the family ethic and its gender division of labor by stigmatizing nontraditional families and by pushing women (except welfare mothers) to return to their "rightful" place in the home.

The family ethic is the ideological glue that continues to reinforce the gender division of labor. Women are locked into traditional domestic roles and forced to remain financially, if not emotionally, dependent on men. The belief that women belong at home rationalizes the conditions that produce the economic vulnerability that keeps them there. In other words, women's presence in the home appears to "prove" that home is where women want to be and where they belong.

Social reproduction is the final source of gender inequality, and is another concept that is particularly emphasized in socialist feminist analyses of the welfare state.[4] Social reproduction refers to the way societies meet individual needs; prepare the next generation for school, work, marriage, and parenthood; and replace those who die. While many institutions play a role in social reproduction, in Western capitalist societies it is routinely expected to take place in two-parent, heterosexual homes.

The gender division of labor defines social reproduction as "women's work." Even women who work outside the home are expected to reproduce the species (procreation), to rear and socialize children so that they comply with social norms and expectations (childrearing), to purchase and prepare food, clothing, and shelter (homemaking), and to provide for family members who are too old or young to care for themselves (caretaking). In other words, women's unpaid labor in the home not only meets the family's physical and emotional needs, but it keeps the economy going by supplying a healthy, productive, and properly socialized labor force.

The concept of social reproduction became central to the socialist feminist analyses for several reasons. First, it highlighted the work women do and the relationship between women, the family, and the labor market. Second, as we will see below, it helped explain the role of the welfare state. And third, as we will see in Part 4, it showed how women's activism could develop.

FEMINIST CRITIQUES AND CORRECTIVES

THE WELFARE STATE GAINED POPULARITY AS A SUBJECT of study in the late 1960s and 1970s, just before the social welfare system that had expanded in the postwar years began to be cut back. At first, most welfare state analyses focused on questions of labor, class, and capitalism. Scholars examined how the welfare state affected and was shaped by economic production, class divisions, and class struggle, but not how it reflected and reinforced social reproduction, the gender division of labor, and women's political struggles.

The feminist critique that was launched in the late 1970s appeared because the existing scholarship ignored these "women's issues." Resisted by male-dominated academia, feminist scholars, like the welfare mothers, had to fight back. Their critique, synthesized below, argues that traditional studies of the welfare state— covering AFDC as well as Social Security, Unemployment Insurance, and most other social programs—failed to consider (1) the roles of women, the family, and social reproduction in the origins of the welfare state; (2) the ways in which social welfare programs enforced the family ethic (as well as the work ethic); (3) the programs' differential treatment of women and men; (4) the re-creation by the welfare state of the gender and race (as well as class) hierarchies found in the wider society; and (5) the role of patriarchy in the construction of the welfare state.

The feminist critique of traditional welfare state theories was derived from the three feminist perspectives noted earlier. This review relies most heavily on the work of the socialist feminists, however, and to a lesser extent on that of the liberal feminists, because these two approaches examined the relationship between women and the welfare state in more depth than the cultural feminists. My synthesis of feminist theory, as well as the theoretical section of Part 4, represents the condensation of a very complex body of work and does not identify individual scholars (except in the notes). Such a broad overview inevitably oversimplifies many issues, pays inadequate attention to important debates among feminist thinkers, and omits many theoretical concerns. Its aim is to highlight some of the major points made and to examine some of the reasons feminist scholars felt compelled to contest the traditional views. (For those seeking a more in-depth look, the notes to this part represent a good starting place.)

BRINGING THE FAMILY IN: THE ORIGINS OF THE WELFARE STATE

THE QUESTIONS OF HOW, WHEN, AND WHY NATIONS create welfare states were addressed in a number of ways by scholars in the 1960s and 1970s. The three main theoretical approaches—liberal, social citizenship, and Marxist—all associated the origins of the welfare state with capitalist development. But while each understood the process somewhat differently, none paid adequate attention to the relationship between women, the family, and the state.

Liberal social science linked the development of the welfare state to the new forms of economic insecurity created by the Industrial Revolution.[5] While the emerging market economy improved the overall standard of living, it also created economic hazards that few individuals had the power to control. For one, the mechanization of industry impoverished some workers and rendered others superfluous. Families risked losing their income-earners due to old age, illness, disability, and unemployment, as well as the absence or death of a breadwinner. The forces of industrialization left wage earners dependent on the decisions of an employer, the condition of the local labor market, and the vagaries of the larger economy.

Along with these new sources of economic vulnerability, the growth of crowded cities, the influx of impoverished immigrants, and rapid social change generated a myriad of social problems whose management exceeded the capacity of families, relief systems, and other existing mechanisms of support.

The mounting problems of living and working in an industrial society gradually elicited a government response. Once a nation developed an economic surplus and organizational capacity, the government gradually created new social welfare institutions to shield workers from the worst abuses of the labor market and to compensate them for such catastrophes as the loss of a job or a work-related injury. Along with private charities and voluntary organizations, the state also began to absorb more and more of the economic, educational, public health, and social service functions that had been performed by families and other local institutions. The expanding social welfare system not only helped to regulate the uncertain labor market, but also helped to stabilize the wider social order. These new programs, although never enough and often accompanied by too much social control, nevertheless improved the quality of life for many people.

The second theoretical approach to the rise of the welfare state—the social citizenship model—also holds that the move from pre-industrial to industrial society undercut traditional mechanisms of community support and created the need for new ones.[6] However, this approach argues that the need for "social integration," rather than protection against economic risk, was the prime reason for the development of the welfare state. The achievement of social integration and solidarity, however, depended on the full participation of all members of society, and this participation in turn required the acquisition of the rights of citizenship: civil rights (the right to individual liberty and equality before the law, upheld by legal institutions); political rights (the right to vote and to run for office, based in political institutions); and social rights (the right to a minimum standard of living, lodged in the welfare state). The welfare state emerged after workers struggled for civil and political rights and used these hard-won gains to demand greater economic security in the form of social rights (welfare state benefits).

Over time, the scale and scope of these rights widened and came to cover more groups: civil and political rights that were initially restricted to male landowners were extended to working and middle class men (and later to women). Similarly, social rights that were initially restricted to the poor were gradually granted to these other groups. However, the pace and extent of this expansion of social rights—that is, the growth of the welfare state—varied widely throughout Western capitalist nations, with the U.S. welfare state being one of the slowest and most meager.

Looking at the same history, traditional (pre-feminist) Marxists argued that the welfare state arose to protect capitalism from itself, rather than as an inevitable response to mounting social problems or to the enfranchisement of the masses.[7] The welfare state's development therefore reflects the interaction of three factors: industrial capitalism's need for a more efficient environment in which to operate—in particular, the need for a highly productive labor force; the struggle of the working class against exploitation; and the recognition by the propertied class that welfare programs are the price that must be paid for political stability. More specifically, the welfare state emerged to maintain the conditions necessary for profitable capital accumulation and the maintenance of social order—both of which can be jeopardized by the dynamics of capitalist production. On the one hand, capitalist profits depend heavily on the laboring capacity of workers. On the other hand, capitalists cannot be relied upon to reproduce and maintain the labor force because their profits depend on low wages, high rates of unemployment, and spending as little as possible on benefits or the work environment.

The tension between the capitalists' drive for profits and the workers' need to survive periodically threatens the productivity, if not the existence, of the workforce. When the clash between making profits and meeting human needs creates undue economic inefficiency or deep political conflict, the state often steps in, using social welfare programs to mediate the conflict. The health services, educational programs, and income-support benefits that are introduced in times of economic or political instability (as well as under other conditions) have strengthened capitalism by using the power of the state to create the conditions necessary for profitable investment, increased consumption, and social harmony.

From the perspective of the feminists who began investigating welfare in the late 1970s, the three standard explanations for the rise of the welfare state lacked a gender analysis: they minimized the importance of the family, sexist bias, and gender inequality, and failed to discuss the role that middle- and working-class women activists had played in the development of the welfare state—a subject that we will return to in Part 4.[8]

Given their interest in women, it is not surprising scholars holding all the feminist perspectives spotted the perfunctory treatment of the family in the traditional analyses of the origins of the welfare state. For instance, traditional liberal theory recognized that the government became involved in social welfare to back up families and other local systems of support that, due to the advance of industrialization, could no longer carry out all the tasks assigned to them. However, due to its preoccupation with the role of the state in protecting workers against the weaknesses of the labor market, liberal welfare state theory did not adequately situate workers in the home. Social citizenship theory's emphasis on citizenship downplayed the family in similar ways. When the family did come into the picture, it was as an afterthought, rather than as an analytic variable built into the general theory.

Traditional Marxism also gave inadequate attention to the family, and to the position of women in society in general. Reflecting its preoccupation with the production side of the equation, Marxism took women's role in the daily and intergenerational reproduction and maintenance of the working class as a given, and failed to examine the family as the site of social reproduction. Although Frederick Engels saw that women suffered as the property of men and equated women's domestic labor with "slavery," he concluded that this would change once women entered the wage labor force and after workers transformed capitalism into a socialist society.

The failure of the three traditional analyses to recognize that "families mattered" in the development of the welfare state helps explain the lack of attention to the role of social reproduction and to women's unpaid labor in the home. Socialist feminists in particular argued that the welfare state arose not only to cushion the adverse impact of industrialization (liberal theory), to foster social solidarity (social citizenship theory), and to mediate the conflict between production for profit and production for need (Marxist theory), but also to underwrite the cost of social reproduction in the home. In other words, when the imperatives of profitable production—high profits, low wages, and a degree of unemployment—came into conflict with the requirements of social reproduction, the average family's need for adequate resources to carry out its assigned caretaking and maintenance tasks forced the state to step in to shore up it up economically. In subsidizing the family and women's unpaid labor in the home, the state helped families. But it also reinforced both the family ethic and the work ethic, and thus perpetuated the economic dependence of women on men.

Bringing families into the analysis in this way led to a reconsideration of the origins of the welfare state. Socialist feminists concluded that those standard theories that tied the rise of the welfare state to the loss of family functions were unknowingly portraying the impact of industrialization on patriarchal arrangements in the home. Prior to industrialization, the laws of marriage, property, inheritance, and public assistance placed nearly all authority in the hands of the male head of household. However, the forces of capitalist development—increased geographic mobility, smaller families, greater dependence on market wages, the employment of women, and the attachment of rights to individuals rather than family units—shattered the established bases of male domination, both inside and outside the home. While traditional analyses argued that the welfare state arose to replace the functions of the family that industrialization had undermined, socialist feminists pointed out that social welfare programs were effectively replacing private patriarchy, based on individual male authority in the home, with public patriarchy, grounded in collective control by men through the state.

GENDER BLIND: THE DIFFERENTIAL TREATMENT OF WOMEN AND MEN

THE SECOND FEMINIST CRITIQUE OF THE STANDARD welfare state theories focussed on the different ways that social programs treat women and men, and the sexism this perpetuates.[9] As a result of their concerns about sex discrimination in general, liberal feminists were among the first to discover that conventional social welfare theories were gender blind: the liberal, social citizenship, and Marxist discussions of social welfare, like social policy itself, all presumed a male standard based on waged work as the norm for all welfare state recipients, and then generalized their findings to all women (and men of color)—as if race and gender differences did not exist. Because of this, and despite their different foci, each of the traditional theories presented an inaccurate picture of women's relationships to the welfare state.

One male bias found in both liberal and social citizenship theory stemmed from the twin premises that (1) waged work is the prime way to contribute to society and (2) social welfare policy exists to protect workers and their families from the risk of lost income or to compensate those who have contributed to society but are without financial support through no fault of their own. The presumption was that welfare state participants were male breadwinners and that women were dependents of men; at the same time, the ways in which the gender division of labor keeps women from qualifying for the more substantial welfare state benefits were obscured.

Although the standard theories looked at the relationship between the welfare state and the labor market, they all failed to

Food and clothing being distributed at the Surplus Commodities Distribution Center in Springfield, Masachusetts, 1938. Note the sign on the left which indicates that even in the WPA, the traditional two-parent family ethic was upheld vigorously. [National Archives]

recognize that wage and employment structures were gendered in ways that penalized female recipients. For example, liberal feminists pointed out that because Social Security and Unemployment Insurance benefits are wage-based, women receive lower benefits than men. By not compensating for the male/female wage gap, which is the result of sex discrimination in the labor market, the welfare state reproduces it. Second, feminists showed that it is harder for women to receive full benefits because of the ways in which the programs are employment-driven. Given their caretaking duties, women have a harder time than most men accumulating the ten years of work experience needed to qualify for Social Security retirement benefits. Similarly, Unemployment Insurance does not cover most of the part-time, temporary, or intermittent jobs that many women "choose" in order to care for their families. Nor does it cover the husband or wife who leaves his or her job to follow a spouse to a new city—a pattern much more common among women than men. Finally, the discussion of the risks of the labor market found in these theories presumes that most workers are men: pregnancy, childrearing, and caretaking responsibilities are rarely considered. These risks, like sexual harassment and sex-seg-regated jobs, are faced primarily by women. Women need protection from these and other failures of the labor market. They also need protection from failures of marriage (such as divorce, deser-tion, lack of child support from a noncustodial parent, and vio-lence in the home), all of which may impoverish women and leave them to raise children on their own.

The social citizenship analysis of the social welfare system also failed to consider the male biases in its definition of citizenship.[10] More specifically, the theory accepted past and present measures of social citizenship—the capacity to bear arms, to own property, or to work in paid employment—that exclude women. Moreover, it uncritically defined the self- supporting white male wage-earner as the "ideal citizen" and argued that an individual's rights, identity, and social status are established by ties to the labor market. Rarely did the theory consider that these rules of citizenship exclude eco-nomically dependent individuals, including both women whose independence has been circumscribed by their economic depen-dence on men and African-American men and women whose inde-pendence has been circumscribed by racism. Nor did it consider other important sources of rights, identity, and status, such as a person's role in the family and community.

The social citizenship theory privileges (white) men in still another way by arguing that the development of the welfare state (or social rights) depended on the working class's prior acquisi-tion—through political struggle—of civil and political rights. This understanding of history ignores the fact that women, people of color, and other politically disenfranchised groups have had less and subordinated access to civil and political rights. Nor does it explain how women in the United States played a major role in the development of the welfare state before they won the vote in 1919.

Feminists pointed out that the (male) concept of citizenship places women in a double bind. Women have to demand the social rights of citizenship on the grounds of equality (i.e., on equal terms with men) or on the grounds of difference (i.e., based on their different talents, needs, and responsibilities "as women"). In the first instance they end up as "lesser men," because in patriarchal societies women lack equal opportunity to compete for jobs, income, prestige, and power. In the second instance they risk less than full recognition, because patriarchal society devalues women's identity, status, and contributions.

The male bias in traditional Marxist theory stemmed from the priority it gave to class over patriarchal power. The early Marxists, who predated the modern welfare state in Europe and the United States, argued that women became oppressed when capitalism turned them into male property.[11] They argued that the exploitation of women and men derived from the same source, and assumed that their oppression could be understood in the same terms. Thus the entry of women into the workforce would lead to their emancipation not simply by reducing their economic dependence on men, but by engaging them in the struggle to transform capitalism and eliminate the private property on which their subordination was based.

The contemporary Marxists who studied the modern welfare state carried this gender-blind analysis forward.[12] They analyzed who benefits and who loses from the class organization of the social welfare system, but they seldom asked who benefits and who loses from the ways in which society organizes the reproduction of the labor force, the consumption of goods and services, and the rearing of the children—that is, who benefits and who loses from the division of labor by gender. Failing to acknowledge the power of patriarchy independent of capitalism, they rarely took up issues of women's oppression, gender differences, or the gendered features of the welfare state.

TWIN DYNAMICS: THE WORK ETHIC AND THE FAMILY ETHIC

THE THIRD FEMINIST CRITIQUE OF TRADITIONAL WELFARE state theories targeted their singular preoccupation with the work ethic. Traditional approaches not only assumed that all workers were men, but also devoted a great deal of their analysis to the relationship between welfare state benefits and market wages. Liberal theorists argued that welfare state benefits were below the lowest prevailing wage so that no one would choose public assistance or social insurance benefits over low-paid work. Social citizenship analysts added that, in varying degrees, Western industrial nations kept benefits down in order to reduce the leverage of workers vis-à-vis capital and to weaken their capacity to bargain for higher wages. Marxists argued that meager social welfare benefits increased the size of the labor pool, held wages down, kept workers in line, and otherwise enabled capital to exploit labor.

Parts 1 and 2 have already described some of the ways in which public assistance programs reinforced the work ethic by keeping women off AFDC/TANF and thus tied to the labor market. Other social welfare programs, such as Social Security and Unemployment Insurance, also reinforce the work ethic by favoring those who have worked or who are considered without work through no fault of their own (such as the young, old, sick, and disabled), while penalizing those deemed able but unwilling to work. But it took feminist theory to show that social welfare programs enforce the family ethic as well.[13] Nearly all feminists agree that in the United States, as in most Western industrial countries, the structure of welfare benefits keeps women economically tied to marriage and the family, and reinforces traditional gender roles. Both liberal and socialist feminists have shown that social welfare programs—including AFDC/TANF, Social Security, and Unemployment Insurance—favor the heterosexual, two-parent family by treating women recipients differently based on their marital status. Thus women who form and sustain traditional households are rewarded and those who depart from prescribed roles are punished. Just as welfare programs ensure that working people do better than those on welfare, so households headed by married or previously married women, such as widows, fare better than households headed by single mothers, abandoned women, or divorced wives, all of whom are considered able but unwilling to marry, and, often, responsible for a family's break up.

Feminists have focussed on the family ethic not only because it adds to women's oppression by enforcing their economic dependence on men, but because it inaccurately assumes that the family is a stable unit whose members pool and distribute their income and power equally.[14] This belief that the family is harmonious and equitable is demonstrably false—one need only look at the nation's high rates of divorce and separation, at the widespread violence against women and children, and at the frequent disputes over rights and responsibilities in the home. To feminists, conflicts within the family are a manifestation of patriarchal power in the same way that conflicts between workers and employers are expressions of the power relations of class.

Feminists of color put forward a slightly different analysis. They pointed out that when it comes to African-American women, the welfare state enforces the work ethic, but violates the family ethic.[15] As we saw in Parts 1 and 2, social welfare policies either excluded African-American women or forced them to work for low wages, even as it encouraged white middle-class women to stay at home. This double standard not only channeled black women into exploitative jobs, but kept them from living according to the rules of the family ethic, if they so desired, by staying home. In other words, welfare state policies, combined with racial discrimination, effectively denied black women the opportunity to choose, as many white women did, to trade the constraints of economic dependence on men for the protections that family life offered to women. This insight was especially important because it showed how the forces of domination work differently in black and white communities: among blacks, the family often functions as a refuge from a racist society and its role as a site of resistance to racial oppression may therefore override the oppression of women that it may also entail.

RECREATING GENDER AND RACE HIERARCHIES

THE FOURTH FEMINIST CRITIQUE OF THE STANDARD welfare state theories focused on the question of domination rather than discrimination—that is, on the way the welfare state recreates gender, race, and class hierarchies rather than its differential treatment of women and men. The standard welfare-state theories all examined power, but only as it pertained to class relations. They thus accepted the two-tiered structure of the welfare state described in Part 1—universal social insurance for the middle class and means-tested public assistance for the poor—as reflecting wider class inequalities. But the liberal and social citizenship theories argued that the protection against the risks of the market economy provided by the welfare state soften these class differences by cushioning poverty and promoting social integration. In contrast, Marxists argued that the welfare state does little to change the unequal distribution of income and wealth, and that because its programs often quiet social unrest, it enforces the power of the ruling class.

Feminists, on the other hand, argued that class is not the only fault line in the welfare state.[16] As we have seen, the welfare state incorporates the family ethic (which supports the economic dependence of women on men), subsidizes social reproduction in the home (based on the division of labor by gender), and rewards men's paid labor in the market over women's unpaid labor in the home. The welfare state therefore actively reinforces the social and economic bases of male domination and female subordination. Since the employment-based distribution of benefits inevitably recreates the inequalities of the labor market, the welfare state rein-

forces the unequal power relations based on the differential treatment of workers based on gender.

The two-tiered structure of the welfare state also reproduces
the inequalities of race found in wider society because the more
disadvantaged members of society—those who are more likely to
be deprived of an adequate income by racial discrimination—are
relegated to the stigmatized and locally administered public assistance programs. Since these programs serve those who have not
been able to work during their prime years due to illness, disability, lack of marketable skills, or childrearing responsibilities, the
poor, women, and people of color are overrepresented on their
rolls. Further, to the extent that both employment and social welfare benefits are based on a person's citizenship status, this extends
to immigrants, including the growing number of foreign-born persons of color.

WHAT ABOUT PATRIARCHY AND GENDER OPPRESSION?

THE PRECEDING FEMINIST CRITIQUES TARGETED A MIX OF
liberal and socialist feminist concerns about the lack of attention
to women and the family in the scholarship on the welfare state,
its unfair treatment of women relative to men, its support for traditional two-parent families and stereotypical gender roles, and its
ability to reproduce the hierarchies of gender and race as well as
class. The final critique shifts the focus from the impact of the welfare state on the lives of women to the relationship between the
welfare state and the dynamics of capitalism and patriarchy. This
critique, which came from the socialist feminists, went through
several stages, or what I will call here conversations. The first
defined the welfare state as an institution that oppressed and subordinated women by reinforcing patriarchal controls. The second
argued that the welfare state mediates conflicts between capitalism
and patriarchy. Building on the insights of both, the third added
that the welfare state has the potential to emancipate as well as to
control women. It is useful to review these conversations not only

because they show the development of the feminist analysis of the welfare state, but because the last conversation sets the stage for moving on from our analysis of the struggle of feminists in the academy to the struggle of women in the streets.

Conversation 1: Reinforcing Patriarchy. Feminist theorists uncovered the patriarchal underpinnings of the welfare state early on and showed how its policies fostered the oppression of women.[17] They developed their theory about the role of patriarchy by studying the social welfare system itself. One of their first insights was that social policy typically defines women in terms of their biological functions, and uses state power to "protect" women as reproducers of the species and socializers of the next generation. For example, during the Progressive Era many states passed labor laws to protect women on the grounds that poor working conditions jeopardized their capacity to bear and rear children. Despite repeated efforts, social reformers failed to get these laws—which shortened the work day, limited night shifts, restricted the number of pounds a worker could lift, and mandated that employers provide seats—extended to men, who also needed protection from unsafe jobs. Two other programs that were enacted at the same time as the protective labor laws—the Mothers' Pensions discussed in Part 2 and the Shepphard Towner Maternal and Child Health Act of 1921 (an early federal public health nursing program for mothers and children)—also defined women as childbearers and childrearers who needed "protection" from the labor market.

These early efforts did little to alleviate gender oppression. Many employers used the protective labor laws as an excuse not to hire women, to pay them lower wages, or to send them back home. As we saw in Part 1, Mothers' Pensions evolved into ADC, which, as a program for single women only, was highly vulnerable to attack; the Shepphard Towner program lasted only a few years before Congress closed it down.

The Social Security Act of 1935 perpetuated the biological construction of womanhood by serving most women as mothers

Applying for welfare, New York City, 1985. [George Cohen/Impact Visuals]

and wives, and by assisting them primarily when they were caring for children or spouses. For example, for many years the AFDC program did not aid a pregnant woman until her child was born. Similarly, Medicaid did not cover pregnant women until Congress added maternity benefits in 1980. To this day, a single woman on AFDC/TANF and a surviving spouse under age sixty-five on Social Security lose benefits when their youngest children reach the age of eighteen. This "widow's gap" leaves adult women who do not have spouses or children without any governmental income support unless they qualify for benefits as disabled or become eligible for local home relief.

The conversation about reinforcing patriarchy also showed how welfare state programs shore up patriarchal controls by perpetuating the economic dependence of women on men.[18] Until 1970, when the women's movement forced the courts to override the policy on the grounds of discrimination, Social Security rules made it difficult for a working woman to claim Social Security benefits for a dependent male spouse: it had to be proven that the husband's earnings had supplied less than one-fourth of the couple's income during the year prior to the wife's retirement (or death). Yet the wives of employed men were not required to undergo this "support test." Further, some of the Social Security Act programs do more than presume the economic dependence of women on men—they actively reward it. First, as noted earlier, social welfare programs promote women's economic dependence by penalizing those who challenge the family ethic. The retirement benefits favor one-earner over two-earner couples and lifetime homemakers over working wives. Many women receive a larger benefit as dependent spouses (one-half their husbands' grants) than they can qualify for on the basis of their own work records. As late as 1985, more than one-third of the women who were eligible for benefits based on their own records received them instead as wives or widows of workers because of their lower wages. Working women who have paid into the Social Security system for years complain they gain nothing in retirement that they could not receive "for free" on the basis of their husbands' earnings and that they are no better off than homemakers who have paid no Social Security taxes at all. This would be different if benefits were available to women in their own right, rather than as dependents living in male-headed family units.

Conversation 2: Mediating Conflict. As the second conversation about patriarchy and capitalism commenced, the discussion became more complex. Instead of arguing that the welfare state simply reinforced patriarchal rule, feminists began to see patriarchy and capitalism as two independent systems that could work in concert or as rivals, and that conflicts between them were often mediated by the welfare state.[19]

When the forces of patriarchy and capitalism work in concert, the gender division of labor is enforced, to the advantage of both systems. Take women's labor: women's unpaid work in the home benefits individual men by relieving them of the responsibility for raising children, managing the family's consumption, and maintaining the family in other noneconomic ways. These services are not part of men's gender-assigned roles, and men with resources can even buy them. Wives also meet the personal, sexual, and emotional needs of men, and their commitment to the home keeps them from competing with men for better paying jobs and jobs with more responsibility. The state upholds the home as a refuge for men, but for women it can often mean economic dependence, the double day, or domestic violence.

While "serving" patriarchy, this gendered family arrangement also "serves" capitalism. For one, women at home become a flexible pool of workers who can be pulled in and out of the labor force as needed—to fill labor shortages, to compete with male workers, and to otherwise lower labor costs by pushing, or keeping, wages down. Women's unpaid labor in the home also ensures the maintenance of the current and future labor force. Finally, employers use the fact that women have family responsibilities to justify hiring them in low-paid, sex-segregated jobs, which once again benefits capitalism by keeping wages down and benefits patriarchy by keeping women economically insecure. As we have seen, when families cannot survive on what they earn, welfare can shore them up so that they will continue to carry out the social and reproductive tasks on which both systems depend.

In the tug of war over women's labor, the two systems also create many conflicts within and between themselves. For example, as industrial capitalism advanced, its demand for low-paid workers drew more and more women out of the home. Once women became permanent members of the workforce, they were no longer the reserve army that could be brought into the labor market at will to drive wages down. Having achieved a critical mass, working women joined unions and otherwise mobilized against the inequality of opportunity and rights on the job and in wider society.[20] In addition to both serving and challenging capitalist control, the employment of women weakened patriarchal controls in the home. Working wives deprived individual men of women's domestic services and increased women's economic autonomy.

Instead of simply "servicing" capitalism or patriarchy separately, feminists concluded the welfare state helps to mediate the competing demands for women's home and market labor. One way it does this is by categorizing women as "deserving" and "undeserving" of aid based on their marital status. We have seen how some social welfare programs (like AFDC/TANF) send poor and working-class women into the workforce, while others (like Old Age Insurance) encourage middle-class wives and mothers to stay home. This suggests that the welfare state tries to reconcile the imperatives of both systems so that each is served, at least in part. These mediation efforts fall especially hard on African-American women, who are more likely than white women to end up with low and stigmatized benefits.

The welfare state mediates the conflicting demands of capitalism and patriarchy as well when women become organized and force the government to address their need for labor laws, equal pay, a minimum wage, childcare, family leave, educational rights, and greater control over their bodies. That many of these demands remain only partially fulfilled, and are now threatened across the board, suggests the extent of the resistance to women challenging domination at home and exploitation on the job.

Conversation 3: Emancipating Women. The third conversation about the welfare state moved from defining it as instrument of mediation to seeing it as arena of political struggle. Once it became clear that some welfare state policies could weaken the power of patriarchy and capitalism, feminists realized that welfare was an institution that both regulated the lives of women and created the conditions for their emancipation. Drawing on studies by the social citizenship school, which showed the differential effect of meager and generous welfare systems on the power of their recipients, these feminists concluded that the welfare state can serve the interests of dominant and subordinate groups at different times and in different ways, and that welfare programs can therefore have both regulatory and emancipatory possibilities.[21]

The social citizenship theorists maintain that access to social welfare benefits is an important source of power because it enables workers to subsist without having to rely fully on the market, and that this reduced vulnerability to employers has the potential to increase workers' power vis-à-vis capital and even to alter class relations. Feminists recognize this dynamic but point out that it operates differently for those who need to gain full access into the market in the first place. This not only means equal opportunity but equal pay for comparable work, equal voice in the workplace, and the caretaking supports needed to balance work and family responsibilities. Having once become full-fledged players in the market, women can then use welfare state benefits to enhance their political leverage, helping them to negotiate for decision-making power in the workplace.

But even this will not be enough as women still have to negotiate for power in the home as well. Just as cash benefits can increase a worker's leverage in the market, so they can increase a woman's leverage at home and thereby lessen the hold of patriarchy as well as capitalism. By reducing women's financial vulnerability, the welfare state can free women to bargain, individually and collectively, with men, and to enter and leave relationships on their own terms. Even more critically, public programs can contribute to women's emancipation by enabling them to maintain independent households thereby allowing them true autonomy. If the welfare state were to develop in these ways, it could free women from economic dependence on men and markets, embolden them to take risks at home and on the job, and alter gender as well as class relations.

This proposal remains controversial even among feminists, however. Some argue that women who accept welfare benefits exchange dependence on men for dependence on the state—and remain poor because welfare benefits are so low. Others argue that while dependence on men isolates women, dependence on the state brings them together, both as clients and as employees.[22] Their shared poverty and status as recipients can create the basis for collective action among welfare recipients and workers—if not together, then independently. In Part 4, we will examine the activism of poor, working, and middle-class women-both white women and women of color—to show how they first turned the basic need for food, clothing, and shelter, and then the welfare state itself, into an arena of political struggle.

PART FOUR

Fighting Back: From the Legislature to the Academy to the Streets

WHEN YOU HEAR THE WORD ORGANIZER, LEADER, REBEL, or participant, what type of person comes to mind? These words typically evoke images of white men because for centuries most people believed that women did not, and should not, fill these activist roles.[1] It was not that women were not activists, however, but that their activism was hidden. The traditional, liberal, social citizenship, and Marxist theories all addressed social conflict and, despite their different interpretations, they consistently located political struggle within established organizations, movements, and institutions, all of which excluded women. Having failed to look for, much less locate, women's activism where it in fact took place, they found few women activists. They then decided that this must mean that women are conservative, politically unmotivated, and thus unworthy of study. This exclusion of women from the traditional scholarship on activism not only distorts the historical record, but disempowers women by denying them knowledge of an important part of their heritage.

The liberal political theorists dealt with the role of social conflict by minimizing it. They argued that industrialization eliminated the most basic sources of tension between workers and employers, and generated the political mechanisms needed to resolve the new conflicts that emerged.[2] It was not that discord disappeared, but that technology narrowed the economic gap between the haves and have-nots, and generated a set of political institutions and a shared body of ideas, beliefs, and values that effectively replaced class conflict. The welfare state emerged naturally from a process of mediating conflict, the result of agreement among diverse social groups that social welfare provision was necessary to protect and compensate individuals and families for the risks they incurred while living and working in a market economy. The social citizenship theorists agreed that welfare state benefits were won politically. Less interested than their liberal counterparts in showing that democratic societies have no need for class conflict and more willing to acknowledge the role of "pressure from below," they suggested that political conflict was in fact critical to the development of the welfare state.[3] As we saw in Part 3, their analysis held that social rights (e.g., social welfare programs) emerged from political struggles that were in turn predicated on earlier successful battles for legal and political rights. Having fought for and won these democratic rights of citizenship, male workers insisted on economic security, which included a government-protected, minimal standard of living. Governments responded to the pressure by smoothing out the rough edges of capitalism and ensuring that market inequality did not undermine economic stability, political harmony, and social solidarity. To the extent that these hard-won social welfare benefits had the potential to insulate workers against market forces and provide them with leverage in their struggles with employers, they became a power resource that could embolden workers individually and collectively to take the risks involved in fighting economic exploitation.

The traditional Marxist theorists focused more directly on conflict as class struggle, which they argued arose from the contradictions of capitalism. One of these contradictions—the contradiction between the private nature of profitable production and the "social" character of work—made collective action possible.[4] This is because the continued accumulation of capital moved economic production to ever larger factories, thereby bringing workers together in one place and exposing them to their shared exploitation and a common enemy. A second contradiction—that between production for profit and production for need—also created the potential for collective action. As we saw in Part 2, profitable capital accumulation requires certain levels of unemployment to keep profits up and labor costs down. Because this leads to an unequal distribution of income and wealth and deprives workers of an adequate standard of living, it periodically stimulates demands for higher wages, government regulation of the market, and greater access to political power. To forestall such turmoil, business and government may try to repress striking workers and popular movements, or they may try to diffuse the unrest by meeting at least some of the workers' needs. The resulting reforms become the building blocks of the welfare state. But the outcome of this struggle is neither inevitable nor predetermined; it is the result of a contest between the demands of capital and those of popular movements, as mediated by the state.

THE FEMINIST CORRECTIVE

THE DISCUSSION OF SOCIAL CONFLICT IN ALL THREE traditional theories focused on established political institutions-primarily trade unions, electoral parties, social movements, and the state—and therefore missed the activism of women, which often took place in other arenas. It was only when feminists began to investigate the "spaces" that women inhabit—their clubs, auxiliaries, workplaces, unions, and social networks—that they dis covered a long and inspiring history of activism. White middle-class women's activism surfaced first because most scholars expected these women to be the most important and because privileged women left behind the kinds of materials—letters, diaries, and organizational files—that historians depend on to piece the past together. Gradually, however, feminists began to capture the collective activism of working women,[5] community-based homemakers,[6] and welfare state clients,[7] as well as that of the middle-class reformers who worked in women's organizations and large-scale women's movements.

As they uncovered women's activism, feminist scholars began to see how the gender division of labor structures the activism of men and women differently. Although both men and women become active when the contradictions between economic production and social reproduction (described in Part 3) prevent them from carrying out their gendered obligations, the locus of their activism is different. The standard male-oriented theories presumed that all political struggle takes place at the point of production and therefore focused on workplace issues. Workers typically took action through their unions—for instance, when low wages and unsafe working conditions prevented them from performing their breadwinning responsibilities. But feminists found that women also engaged in struggle at the point of consumption.[8] Women, especially working-class women, became active when they were not able to secure the food, clothing, shelter, or other resources they needed to carry out their homemaking and caretaking responsibilities. To carry out their socially assigned tasks, women engaged in collective protest at local grocery stores, housing agencies, and welfare offices. Because this activism was often sporadic, sometimes spontaneous, not always highly organized, and rarely sustained, many scholars and political pundits had dismissed it as politically insignificant. However, as the French historian George Rudé reminds us, under certain conditions small everyday collective actions can have far-reaching effects and can create unanticipated possibilities for social change.[9]

The following account of middle- and working-class women's activism "at the point of consumption" is far from complete. Nevertheless, it will provide us with an important glimpse of the collective actions taken by women of different classes and races, and the relationship between their concerns and the expanding welfare state. Even before the advent of substantial government aid, women were active when their families needed food, clothing, and shelter, or economic and racial justice. As the state increasingly underwrote the costs of social reproduction in the home, women began to target the welfare state. The gender division of labor, the tasks of social reproduction, and in some cases the shared status of being "on welfare" encouraged women to unite to enforce their rights. Thus women turned both their communities and the welfare state into arenas of political struggle.

MIDDLE-CLASS WOMEN TAKE ACTION

THE GENDER DIVISION OF LABOR THAT SENT MEN INTO the labor market and isolated women in their homes led directly to the exclusion of women from the male sphere of formal politics. The social networks and female "culture" that then developed among women were highly supportive of social activism and social reform.[10] In the years before the Civil War, women could not vote or join political parties, but religious and "moral reform" activities were considered suitable. Evangelist revivals swept the nation beginning in the 1820s, becoming one of the earliest "movements" to draw women out of the home. Although the revivals were led by men, women filled the churches, published the religious tracts, and founded the Sunday schools. Women also created roles for themselves in the moral reform movement that evangelism encouraged. For example, driven by notions of female moral superiority, the New England American Female Moral Reform Society (which claimed 445 auxiliaries) and other such organizations worked to rehabilitate prostitutes and eliminate sin. Women also played leading roles in the abolition and temperance movements, as well as in organizations that assisted the poor and mentally ill.

After the Civil War, white middle-class women became active in charity associations, government boards, and the suffrage movement. From 1870 to 1900, they joined the National Women's Suffrage Association and the more conservative American Women Suffrage Association, and conducted 480 campaigns in thirty-three states. The Women's Christian Temperance Union (WCTU) drew even more women into the militant fight against alcohol and saloons, arguing that male drinking depleted household funds. By 1900, the WCTU had over 168,000 dues-paying members in 7,000 locals in forty-eight states.

In addition, scores of women attended the art and literature discussions organized by the women's clubs that proliferated beginning in the late 1860s.[11] By the 1890s, these clubs had coalesced into a national organization, the General Federation of Women's Clubs (GFWC). By 1911, GFWC-affiliated clubs had involved women in cultural, civic, and social welfare activities in towns and cities in all forty-eight states. Women also founded the National Consumers' League (1890s), the Congress of Mothers (1897), the Women's Trade Union League (1903), new suffrage organizations, neighborhood settlement houses, and many other social welfare and civic organizations.

With its ties to the grassroots, this network of women and organizations suggested the direction that activism would take among white middle-class women. Barred from careers in academia, business, and the professions, many educated women carved out an area of expertise as social reformers.[12] By the early 1900s, these women had expanded their arena of responsibility from the home to the larger community. Some groups, led by the National American Women's Suffrage Association (NAWSA) and the National Women's Party (NWP), believed that women should be treated as equals with men and therefore focused nearly exclusively on women's rights, especially the vote (finally won in 1919). Other groups believed that working women and mothers of young children needed special protection because they differed from men,[13] and led small and large battles against slums, dirty milk, and child labor, and for clean cities, decent housing, health insurance, shorter work days, and the minimum wage. These women justified their own activism with the argument that their socialization left them better equipped than men to look out for the welfare of humanity and especially suited for "municipal housekeeping"— a word they often used for social reform. Referred to today as "maternalists," members of this network staffed the settlement houses, supported trade unions, and engaged in a wide range of research, lobbying, and community work. Some, such as Julia Lathrop, the first director of the Children's Bureau, moved into important public posts. Many of these white women and their spiritual descendants carried the reform tradition forward when they worked for Franklin Roosevelt and the New Deal in the 1930s.

African-American women were also active reformers.[14] If gender segregation fostered female social reform organizations among white women, racial segregation forced African Americans to form their own networks. The mobilization of black women had deep roots in the church and drew on the tradition of slave women's networks, free black women's associations, and anti-slavery work. Driven by "duty" and "obligation to the race," black women organized on behalf of what they referred to as "racial uplift," i.e., charity, self-improvement through social service, education, and progress. Before the Civil War, black church women raised funds, organized voluntary missionary societies, and taught Sunday school. Free African-American women also participated in black-led anti-slavery, suffrage, and temperance organizations, and occasionally those organized by whites, although they frequently encountered hostility and outright exclusion. After the Civil War, middle-class African-American women worked to bring resources to the thousands of emancipated but impoverished former slaves, most of whom lived in the rural South. Almost every black women's organization worked to alleviate one or more of the many social problems afflicting an increasingly urban, impoverished, politically powerless, and segregated black population.

By the turn of the century, black people were suffering rampant racial repression: lynching, white primaries, race riots, and urban poverty. In response to the deteriorating condition of "the race," black women established at least as many voluntary associations as their white counterparts, and possibly even more, although they lacked similar resources or political connections. Nonetheless, this network of women's clubs, church organizations, and mutual-aid societies provided the foundation for powerful national organizations, including the National Association of Colored Women (NACW), founded in 1896. By 1914, the NACW represented 50,000 middle-class, educated black women in twenty-eight federations and over 1,000 clubs. The NACW platform ranged from anti-lynching campaigns to refuting negative stereotypes of black women as sexually loose to fighting for women's suffrage and other social reforms. Its members helped their communities establish separate educational and healthcare facilities, settlement houses, and social service organizations. The women in the NACW were also instrumental in the formation of the National Association for the Advancement of Colored People (NAACP) in 1910 and the National Urban League in 1911. Others joined the women's arm of the more separatist Universal Negro Improvement Association (UNIA), headed by Amy Jacques Garvey, Marcus Garvey's wife. Like their white counterparts, black women later worked in the New Deal. For instance, the National Council of Negro Women, formed by Mary McLeod Bethune in 1935, became the most important black women's lobby in Washington, D.C., and Roosevelt appointed Bethune head of the Office of Minority Affairs in the National Youth Administration at a time when few blacks of either gender held high political office.

There was a potential for cooperation between the white and black women's networks because both espoused maternalist values, endorsed a strict work ethic, and promoted services for the poor. But these shared values could not overcome the racial divide. While white women's organizations ignored the issue of race, it was the central issue for the African-American women reformers, who believed that race, poverty, and gender were inextricably intertwined. The black women espoused a maternalism that to a certain extent mirrored that of whites, but they were more accepting of single motherhood and of women having to work outside the home, and therefore opposed making income tests or moralistic behavioral standards prerequisites for government help. They upheld the family ethic not as a behavioral prescription, but because it was a means by which women could claim respect and justice in white America.

Black women's groups occasionally made overtures to white women's organizations, only to be ignored or slighted. For instance, when the white women's organizations prepared an exhibit for the Colombian Exposition at the 1893 Chicago World's Fair, they turned down a request from the black women's clubs to be represented on the board. The next year, the General Federation of Women's Clubs refused to let a well-known black woman—who was representing an established black women's group from Boston—into their convention. Some white suffragists pandered to southern segregationists, arguing that the votes of native-born, educated white women could be used to outweigh those of uneducated blacks in the South and immigrants in the North. Others supported the use of literacy or educational qualifications to reduce the number of such voters. A controversy arose over the participation of black women in a suffrage parade in 1913, and in the early 1920s a major suffrage organization, the National Women's Party, excluded blacks. Even those white women who privately deplored discrimination tacitly accepted the exclusion of African-Americans, and African-American women reformers came to regard their white counterparts with considerable distrust.

What impact did these women, white and black, have on the welfare state? Feminist scholars have answered this question differently. Some have suggested that they institutionalized government intervention on behalf of women and children and therefore helped pave the way for a broader welfare state.[15] Other feminists contend that, although well-intentioned, they left a harmful legacy: for instance, Mothers' Pensions stigmatized single mothers, while employers used protective labor laws to exclude women from better paying jobs.[16] Still others argue that by alleviating the worst miseries of the poor, the reformers stood in the path of more militant demands.[17] In terms of the maternalist strategy itself, some scholars have argued that it idealized motherhood and reinforced women's traditional roles. Others maintain that the women reformers knowingly extolled the virtues of private domesticity in order to legitimize their own activism, which violated prevailing gender norms, and to disarm resistance to their proposals, which called for a greater role for the state.[18] Regardless of the reformers' intent, however, it is generally agreed that they helped create highly gendered notions of women's citizenship on the one hand, and deepened the state's involvement in the private lives of less privileged women on the other.

POOR AND WORKING-CLASS WOMEN RISE UP ANGRY

WORKING-CLASS WOMEN HAD THEIR OWN SOCIAL WELFARE agenda in the late nineteenth and early twentieth centuries, one that arose directly from the conditions of their lives. For instance, many employed women joined unions and demanded better wages and working conditions. In 1909, in one of the more dramatic actions, 20,000 New York City shirtwaist-makers, almost all women (many young and immigrant), staged a militant thirteen-week strike. The "uprising of 20,000," as it became known, forced employers to deal with the newly formed International Ladies' Garment Workers' Union.

In the early twentieth century, as younger single women were becoming militant on the job, mothers and wives—mostly but not entirely immigrants—engaged in collective action in their communities when economic conditions prevented them from carrying out their family responsibilities.[19] For example, they organized food boycotts and rent strikes that were aimed at local merchants and landlords.[20] One of the earliest, the 1902 food boycott, lasted for almost a month. Inside of one day, thousands of women streamed through the streets of New York's Lower East Side, breaking into kosher butcher shops, flinging meat into the streets, and refusing to buy their goods until the prices came down. The protest quickly spread to neighborhoods in Brooklyn and the Bronx. To keep the boycott going, the women called mass meetings, canvassed their neighborhoods, set up picket lines, and raised funds. When, during the protests, 20,000 people gathered for a demonstration, the *New York Times* called for speedy police

Depression-era demonstrators for unemployment insurance. [Culver Pictures]

action against this "dangerous class"—the women, according to the *Times*, "were very ignorant" and "mostly speak a foreign language." The police arrested seventy women and fifteen men.

The 1902 meat boycott was not an isolated event but the forerunner of many other price-driven protests. In 1904, 1907, and 1908, housewives organized rent strikes in New York, Philadelphia, Boston, and Providence, Rhode Island. In 1910, Jewish women in Providence declared war on the kosher butchers, and in August 1914 over 1,000 Italians in Providence took to the streets and brought pasta prices down after shattering a wholesaler's shop windows and throwing his stock of macaroni into the street. World War I price increases sparked militant neighborhood boycotts and mass demonstrations by women in Boston, Chicago,

Philadelphia, and many other cities. The high cost of living drew local women into the Mother's Anti-High Price League, organized by the Socialist Party, which among other things demanded a government response—in this case food assistance. The NACW and NAACP helped lead similar protests in black communities.[21]

The women who took part in these boycotts and strikes turned their status as housewives and their neighborhood networks to good advantage. Although the housewives were not necessarily sympathetic to either trade unions or left politics, they nevertheless felt compelled to take action against the high prices that had eroded their buying power, forced them to work outside the home, and otherwise interfered with their ability to perform their domestic responsibilities. The communities accepted, and even expected, these militant actions because the merchants and landlords were members of the same ethnic groups and as such were expected not to take advantage of their customers. In other words, the assumptions of a "moral economy" in which mutual obligations governed consumption effectively legitimized the boycotts.

The "consumer economy" that replaced this "moral economy" after the First World War created a new set of social expectations for women. Electrification, refrigeration, indoor plumbing, and the telephone transformed housework. To sell new goods and services to a public still wedded to habits of thrift, or too poor to buy much, business and industry built supermarkets, began to extend credit, and advertised.[22] Advertisers portrayed the American standard of living as the model for all families, and targeted women because they were the family shoppers. A "feminine mystique" was created, one that defined housework as an expression of a woman's personality and love of her family, and that linked identity, status, and fulfillment to material acquisition. Convinced by Madison Avenue of the benefits of consumption, women of all classes began to demand more goods and services for their families.[23]

The cost-of-living protests that resumed immediately after the end of World War I were thus driven less by retribution for merchants who had violated the rules of the moral economy than by the discrepancy between the promises of consumerism and the realities of rising prices. The wives of the more skilled and therefore better paid workers were especially frustrated, and some turned to the trade union's women's auxiliaries for help. These auxiliaries, which had begun to support male workers, became a way for women to become involved in the central political, economic, and social questions of the day.

One of the more visible women's auxiliaries was organized in the 1920s by the wives of railroad workers who belonged to the Machinist Union. With chapters in thirty-five states, the District of Columbia, and several Canadian provinces, the machinist's wives demanded a "saving wage," rather than a "living wage," so that they could take advantage of buying on credit to purchase appliances and other products that would enhance their families' standard of living. The wives of the men in the Brotherhood of Sleeping Car Porters, the only black-led union in the country at the time, also wanted to participate in the new consumer culture. The Sleeping Car Porters' auxiliary, which was known as the Women's Economic Council, also assisted families having problems with employers, formed alliances with elite black women, and addressed the black community's concerns about race.

By the mid-1920s, all the more socially conscious women's auxiliaries had begun to call for government-sponsored maternal and healthcare programs for children, for local health departments, and for children's bureaus. In 1928, there were enough active groups for the National Women's Trade Union League (NWTUL), an alliance of working women and middle-class reformers linked to the labor movement, to call the first national conference of trade union auxiliaries.[24]

But the major protest against rising prices and unfulfilled dreams took place in tenant and consumer organizations. These, like the auxiliaries, increasingly targeted the welfare state.[25] Large numbers of women were recruited from the Community Councils for National Defense, created by the federal government to support the war (WWI) effort, as well as from religious groups and the trade union auxiliaries. By May 1919, the Brooklyn Tenant Union (BTU), one of the first tenant advocacy groups, had many of its 4,000 members ready to withhold their rents until increases were rolled back. To make their case, they barricaded themselves into apartments, made speeches from tenement windows, and threatened to pour boiling water on anyone who tried to evict them.

In 1922, the New York Women's Trade Union League (NYW-TUL) founded the Housewives' Industrial League, which called for a public investigation into the health, housing, and other conditions of non-wage-earning women in the home. Mothers in the Communist Party created the United Council of Working-Class Wives to support workplace strikes but soon focussed on the cost of food, fuel, housing, education, and other social welfare issues. Their activities attracted large numbers of non-party women. That same year, the New England Conference of Working-Class Women, representing forty-eight organizations, pledged to fight not only for lower food prices, but also for maternity insurance and an end to child labor.

The collapse of the economy in 1929 led to a new round of community activism. Working-class women found various ways to protect their families from the ravages of the Depression. In rural communities, they exchanged skills, services, clothing, and food, while in urban areas, they began to demand state action. Building on existing networks, housewives in Jewish, Polish, Finnish, Swedish, Irish, Slavic, and African-American communities once again supported strikes, organized consumer boycotts, and blocked evictions. One of the largest consumer actions took place in 1935, when housewives boycotted butcher shops in many large cities, closing some 4,500 in New York City alone. Black working-class women formed their own Housewives' Leagues, launched "Don't Buy Where You Can't Work" campaigns in Baltimore, Chicago, Cleveland, Detroit, New York City, and Washington, D.C., and demanded 75,000 jobs for blacks who had lost theirs during the Depression. In the South, black women joined the

10,000-member interracial Southern Tenant Farmers' Union, which was founded in Arkansas to resist the evictions that began when the Agricultural Adjustment Act paid farmers to destroy crops in order to increase prices. In the end, these "cost-of-living" protests galvanized women in Chicago, Cleveland, Detroit, Los Angeles, Milwaukee, Minneapolis, Newark, Philadelphia, Patterson, St. Louis, Missouri, and Seattle—to name just a few of the places they rose up angry.

In some cities, the uprisings were shortlived. In others, they led to sophisticated organizations—most notably, the Detroit Women's League Against the High Cost of Living, the Chicago United Council Against the High Cost of Living, and the Women's Work Committee of the Washington Commonwealth Federation. The United Council of Working-Class Wives was formed in June 1929 and by 1931 had forty-eight branches in New York City alone. In 1937, as the Depression deepened, its successor, the Progressive Women's Council, led 3,000 women in sit-ins at New York City's twenty-nine largest relief centers, demanding a 40 percent increase in benefits, a cash allowance for clothing, and twenty-four-hour service for emergency cases. This housewife activism peaked in an explosion of protests in the early 1940s after Roosevelt cut social spending in response to conservative critics.[26] The advent of World War II led to a suspension of protest, but huge price increases of 1946–1947 and 1951 sparked two of the largest consumer strikes in U.S. history. The housewives' movement was a national phenomenon in which women politicized the home, the family, and motherhood in unprecedented ways. They increasingly put pressure on the government to regulate the meat and milk industries, to provide decent and affordable housing, and to give them the heath, education, and welfare services they felt they needed to fulfill their gendered obligations. On the one hand, this activism perpetuated women's traditional roles. On the other hand, however, by holding both the system of production and the state responsible for meeting basic human needs, it implicitly endorsed a more radical vision of how society should work.

A WOMAN'S WORK IS NEVER DONE: ACTIVISM AFTER WORLD WAR II

CONTRARY TO POPULAR WISDOM, MIDDLE- AND WORKING-class women remained active after World War II. By this time, however, the "welfare state economy" had begun to shape their efforts. Although virulently anti-government, anti-communist, and anti-feminist attitudes limited what they could accomplish, between 1945 and 1960 many women worked in peace, civil rights, religious, and other organizations. They increasingly held the government responsible for correcting social conditions.[27] One group of women's organizations clustered around the National Women's Party (NWP), which had been founded during the suffrage battle and was the only national women's rights group that remained active in this period. Although the organization shrank dramatically, and became marginalized because it harbored racist, anti-Semitic, and right-wing leanings, it nonetheless continued to press Congress to support an Equal Rights Amendment (ERA), which it had first introduced in 1921.

The second, and much larger, postwar group of women's organizations was allied to the Women's Bureau of the Department of Labor. From the Business and Professional Women to the United Auto Workers' Women's Bureau, these reform-oriented women considered feminism too narrowly focused on women's rights, at the expense of working-class women's concerns. They actively opposed the ERA during the 1940s and 1950s, fearing that it would undercut labor laws that protected employed women. Instead, they continued to argue for pay equity, improved working conditions, and special protection for women on the job.

A third group, closely connected to the second, included women who became active in the Democratic and Republican parties, each of which had a women's division. By the 1950s, women were the backbone of both local and national electoral activity, but they were still locked out of major decision-making roles. Among many other activities, therefore, the women's divisions and their supporters fought to place women in top policymaking posts. They hoped that by presenting lists of qualified women to party leaders, supporting women who were running for elected office, and organizing women into a political constituency, they would improve the status of all women and help transform society.

A fourth group was made up of African-American women. Often unrecognized outside their own communities because the women's movement remained effectively segregated, these women continued to work on issues of central concern to them.

They also played key leadership roles in the civil rights movement. They worked with the National Council of Negro Women, the National Association of Colored Women, and black sororities to protest racial discrimination, although, like white women, they were divided over the ERA, with the National Association of Colored Women in favor and the National Council of Negro Women opposed. They played a major behind-the-scenes role in the Southern Christian Leadership Conference, the church-based organization formed by Martin Luther King, Jr., in 1957, and although they received little credit at the time, it was the Women's Political Council of Montgomery, Alabama, a group of professional black women, that organized the historic Montgomery bus boycott. The 381-day protest—triggered when Rosa Parks, a department store seamstress and secretary of the Alabama NAACP, was arrested for refusing to move to the back of bus—became a critical event in the postwar civil rights struggle.[28] Many black women who later became nationally known leaders started out as local civil rights activists in the late 1950s and early 1960s.[29] They assisted the Freedom Riders, were central to the movement to desegregate public accommodations,[30] and organized voter registration drives, including the one in Mississippi that led to the formation of the Mississippi Freedom Democratic Party (MFDP). Headed by Fannie Lou Hamer, the MFDP delegation to the 1964 Democratic National Convention not only successfully challenged the party but elected the first black legislator in a Southern state. Black women students joined the first sit-ins in the 1960s—a strategy that became the guiding philosophy of the Student Nonviolent Coordinating Committee (SNCC)—and later they created the Black Women's Liberation Committee within SNCC (1964).[31]

In the mid-1960s, white women broke away from the gradualism that characterized the major political parties and the mainstream women's groups to form new feminist organizations, including the National Organization of Women (1967), the Women's Equity Action League (1968), and the National Women's Political Caucus (1971).[32] These "second wave" feminists demanded that the government outlaw sex discrimination and enforce equal rights in employment, education, and healthcare. They also targeted welfare state benefits, and won a minimum wage for domestic workers, greater access to education, admission to most military academies, job protection for pregnant workers, and a woman's right to receive credit on the basis of her own record. It was winning the right to abortion, however, that gave the greatest impetus to the new feminist movement.

In addition, younger, more militant, and mostly white women in the SNCC and Students for a Democratic Society (SDS) began to resist male domination in their organizations and personal lives, and to call for women's liberation, not just women's rights.[33] This insurgency, which crossed race, class, and age lines, led to the creation of the National Conference of Puerto Rican Women (1972), the National Black Feminist Organization (1973), the National Alliance of Black Feminists (1973), the Mexican American Women's Association (1974), the Coalition of Labor Union Women (1974), and the Older Women's League (1980). Each organization targeted its own constituency, however, and the women's movement has continued to be plagued by race, class, and other tensions.

The tumultuous climate of the late 1960s and early 1970s also sparked activism among working-class housewives and single mothers on welfare. In city after city, community-based women began to revive the effort to improve their standard of living. Black, Latina, and white housewives fought against bank redlining and toxic waste dumps, and for rent control, social services, better schools, and safe streets. In the mid-1970s, when fiscal cutbacks threatened neighborhood services, working-class women mobilized against clinic and hospital closings, and demanded better funding for schools. The Congress of Neighborhood Women, founded in 1974 and one of the better-known groups of working-class women, has continued its work.

EARLY WELFARE RIGHTS ORGANIZING: THE NATIONAL WELFARE RIGHTS ORGANIZATION

IN THE 1960S, WOMEN ON WELFARE ALSO BEGAN TO organize in their own interest.[34] Drawing on the long tradition of informal support networks, especially in the black community, these women redefined welfare as a right rather than a privilege, and fought to obtain the benefits to which they were entitled by law. Just as workers employed in factories had discovered their common plight and formed unions to gain strength in numbers, so being "on welfare" provided a basis for women to join forces to protest their meager benefits and the system's controlling rules. While client protest against the welfare system was not new, the welfare rights movement that grew out of these local efforts turned out to be the most significant social protest by poor people since World War II.

The conditions of the mid-1960s—economic prosperity, a liberal political climate, active social movements, political uprisings, and a national war on poverty—created a space in which women on welfare could organize.[35] By this time, the Southern civil rights movement had all but ended and many activists had turned their efforts Northward, drawn by incipient political stirrings among the black urban masses. The 1963 March on Washington and the 1964 War on Poverty focused national attention on economic as well as civil rights issues, as did the twenty-one major riots and civil disorders in 1966, and eighty-three in 1967. The War on Poverty's Community Action Program provided legal and counseling services that helped poor women assert their rights, and with the help of VISTA volunteers, nuns, priests, ministers, and social workers, it facilitated the formation of local welfare rights groups.

The convergence of these forces led George Wiley, a black chemistry professor from Syracuse University and former associate director of the Congress of Racial Equality (CORE), along with other mostly male veterans of the civil rights movement, to form a national welfare rights organization. Its program was based on "A Strategy to End Poverty," a paper written by two academically based social activists, Frances Fox Piven and Richard A. Cloward, that proposed flooding the welfare system with applicants and demands for benefits. Piven and Cloward argued that at least half the families entitled to AFDC never applied, while many others were turned away. They pointed out that welfare departments kept women on welfare uninformed of the range of benefits to which they were entitled, including special grants for clothing and household items, and that if women insisted on what was theirs by law, many more would receive needed financial aid. The resulting surge of applications would also create a fiscal crisis for welfare departments and a political crisis for the Democratic Party. The demand for more welfare dollars would lead big-city Democratic coalitions to split over how to use urban resources and would force the national Democratic Party to put forward a federal solution to poverty that involved the redistribution of income toward the poor.

The formation of a national movement was preceded by growing activity at the local level. In 1963, Johnnie Tillmon, a welfare mother of five, organized Mothers Anonymous in Watts, California; other women formed the Alameda County, California, Welfare Rights organization. The Minneapolis AFDC League, founded in 1964, grew out of a single parents' group at the local YWCA. In 1965, agitation by poor women against welfare cuts led to the Ohio Steering Committee for Adequate Welfare, and in 1966 the Brooklyn Action Welfare Council (B-WAC) was organized after some women attended a welfare rights planning meeting in Washington, D.C. Within a year after the conference, storefront welfare rights centers existed in almost every low-income Brooklyn community. In June 1966, Ohio welfare rights groups staged a 155-mile "Walk for Adequate Welfare" from Cleveland to the state capital in Columbus. National welfare rights planners, led by Wiley, turned this local march into a national media event. They mobilized support for the forty people who set out from Cleveland and for the 5,000 or so others who joined them for some part of the ten-day march. On the last day, simultaneous demonstrations were held in twenty-four cities nationwide, giving official birth to the national welfare rights movement.

In August 1967, the National Welfare Rights Organization (NWRO) held its first national convention, attended by 175 people from forty-five cities in twenty-one states. An organizational structure was set up and Johnnie Tillmon was elected chair. George Wiley, who had earlier been chosen as national director, had already opened the first field office in Washington, D.C. By the time of the convention, the NWRO had 5,000 dues-paying members, concentrated in New York, California, Pennsylvania, Michigan, Virginia, Massachusetts, Ohio, New Jersey, and Illinois. Using a grassroots organizing strategy, it expanded its membership to 22,000 by 1969. The number of local WRO's grew as well, from 130 in twenty-three states in 1966 to 900 in fifty states in 1971.

The NWRO had two main aims: to improve public assistance and to establish a federally guaranteed income. Its organizing strategies ranged from solving individual grievances to collective agitation at welfare offices. Its strategy contributed to the welfare "explosion" of the late 1960s (described in Part 2), and it mounted a militant counteroffensive to welfare cuts in cities in California, New York, Massachusetts, Minnesota, Nevada, New Jersey, and Wisconsin, many of which drew the police and led to arrests. In addition, it lobbied against forced work programs, suitable-home policies, and man-in-the-house rules. Its work transferred millions of dollars to the poor and attracted thousands of women to the welfare rights movement.

Despite positive media coverage and success in mobilizing women across the nation, the NWRO was forced to shift from a street strategy to a political strategy as the times changed. Funding became harder to come by, liberal support diminished, the leadership was co-opted by both politicians and welfare agencies, and the general political climate was more conservative. The organization turned to lobbying against Nixon's Family Assistance Plan (1969–1971), working with local welfare departments to bring about change, and applying for government grants. None of this worked, and in 1975 it declared bankruptcy and closed its doors.

WELFARE RIGHTS BECOMES A WOMEN'S ISSUE

THE 1970s: THE WELFARE RIGHTS MOVEMENT DID NOT disappear, for it had created a sense of entitlement and a cadre of politicized, battle-tested women like Johnnie Tillmon who kept the cause alive. Moreover, in the mid-1970s, a new generation of welfare rights groups surfaced. Unlike the first wave, composed mainly of black women, the second wave included increasing numbers of white women, whose standard of living had fallen due to rising divorce rates and low wages.[36] Influenced by the women's liberation movement, women on welfare—both white women and women of color—began to see welfare as a matter of gender as well as economics.

The first sign of this new wave of activity was in 1972, when the NWRO's women leaders wrested control of the organization. Wiley resigned shortly thereafter and Johnnie Tillmon, an African-American woman, became NWRO's executive director. That same year Tillmon declared, "Welfare is like a traffic accident. It can happen to anybody, but especially it happens to women. And that is why welfare is a woman's issue. For a lot of middle-class women in this country, women's liberation is a matter of concern. For women on welfare it's a matter of survival."[37] Two years later, a group of mostly white feminists organized the Downtown Welfare Rights Action Center (D-WAC) in New York City. Its members (along with groups in New Jersey and elsewhere) argued that welfare was a women's issue because women lacked jobs with good pay; affordable, quality childcare services; and strong income support programs. The number of poor white women attending NWRO's 1974 and 1977 conventions increased, including some young women identified with the feminist and the welfare rights movement.

The more established feminist groups, who played only a minor role in the early welfare rights movement, began to take note of female poverty in the early 1970s. Women from the Women's Equity Action League (WEAL), the Women's Lobby, and the National Organization of Women (NOW) made limited overtures to NWRO.[38] A few Black feminist groups, such as the National Black Feminist Organization and the Coalition of 100 Black Women, also established loose ties to NWRO. In 1976, some mainstream women's groups, along with the Coalition of Labor Union Women (CLUW), National Congress of Neighborhood Women, and Housewives for the ERA, took a stand against President Carter's welfare reform bill because it failed to value women's work at home and because it did not provide for childcare so that a woman could choose to work in or outside the home without penalty. In 1977, the National Council of Women, Work, and Welfare—a coalition that came out of the welfare rights movement—also attempted to mobilize political support for welfare as a women's issue.

These efforts by middle-class feminist groups came too late to significantly influence the welfare reform debate in the early 1970s, especially since the backlash against the War on Poverty and the 1960s social movements was underway. Foreshadowing later disputes, disagreements between the feminists and the NWRO added to the difficulty. While many feminists supported government work programs as a way to help women move out of the home, the NWRO saw these work programs as forced labor which prevented women from choosing where—home or market—they wanted to work. The two groups also disagreed on the ERA. The feminist groups of the 1970s fought hard (if unsuccessfully) to pass the ERA. But the NWRO along with trade-union women opposed the ERA because it undid protective labor laws that benefited working women in low-wage jobs. The male leaders of the NWRO held still another position. They believed that women needed husbands rather than economic independence through work. This stance not only alienated many feminists, but was eventually disavowed by the women leaders of the NWRO as well.

The 1980s: During the 1980s, Ronald Reagan attacked social programs, more states experimented with punitive welfare reforms, and the campaign for the 1988 Family Support Act heated up. This assault, driven by the "austerity economy," reactivated some old welfare rights and advocacy groups with roots in the NWRO and sparked the emergence of new ones. Formed by women on welfare or incorporating them, the groups included: the Coalition for Basic Human Needs in Boston, Massachusetts; Empower in Rochester, New York; Kensington Welfare Rights Union in Philadelphia, Pennsylvania; Kentucky Welfare Reform Coalition; Michigan Welfare Rights Union in Detroit; Parents for Justice in New Hampshire; Reform Organization of Welfare (ROWEL) in St. Louis, Missouri; Welfare Rights Coalition in Cincinnati, Ohio; Welfare Rights Organizing Committee in Seattle, Washington; Welfare Warriors in Long Island, New York; Welfare Warriors in Milwaukee, Wisconsin; Welfare Work and Families Coalition in Chicago, Illinois; and Working for Equality and Economic Liberation (WEEL) in Montana.

Throughout the 1980s these groups developed a repertoire of creative and often militant tactics to protest the mounting cuts in social programs, to demand that welfare meet their needs, and to oppose increasingly coercive work programs. For example, in 1987, the Coalition for Basic Human Needs smashed a cardboard "wall of poverty" at a Massachusetts State House rally, calling for legislation to close the widening gap between monthly benefit checks and the state's cost of living by indexing the grant to inflation. They also attempted a citizen's arrest of the Governor on charges of child abuse for the treatment of the state's poverty-stricken children. The Michigan Welfare Rights Union frequently "turned up the street heat" using civil disobedience to secure fuel and housing for poor women. In 1989, two teams of women toured Southern California to organize Up and Out of Poverty Now campaigns. The travelers exchanged experiences with welfare mothers and helped to stimulate a protest against "welfare fraud sweeps" in Los Angeles.[39]

Other groups that appeared during this period began to organize women on welfare self-consciously as women: ANC Mother's Compton, in Compton, California; California Welfare Mothers in Pacoima, California; Justice, Economic Dignity and Independence for Women (JEDI For Women) in Salt Lake City, Utah; Mothers for Justice in New Haven, Connecticut; Mothers Mobilized for Economic and Social Justice in Ossian, Indiana; Nevada Empowered Women's Project in Reno; Women for Economic Security in Chicago, Illinois; Women's Union in Vermont; Women United in Boulder, Colorado; Women's Economic Agenda Project (WEAP) in Oakland, California; Wise Women in Alaska; and United Single Mothers in Madison, Wisconsin. Besides specifying women in the name of their organization, many of these groups focused on their role as mothers.

Many women on welfare actively identified themselves as mothers and gave highest priority to caring for their children. Reflecting their perception of their gendered obligations, these women insisted that social policy both recognize the value of women's unpaid labor in the home and enable women to feed, clothe, and house their children and otherwise carry out their socially assigned family roles. As mothers, they actively resisted when lawmakers around the country began to force women on welfare to work outside the home. On Mother's Day, in 1989, for example, welfare recipients in Southern California camped out at the state capital both to express solidarity and support for one another and to challenge workfare "so its male-oriented design does not force single parents to abandon family obligations."

Up and Out of Poverty Now campaigns sought to unite people working for wages with people without wages, caring for their children.[40] The emphasis on motherhood departed from the view of some feminist organizations which, while believing in value of women's work in the home, held that fighting for this only reinforced gender stereotypes and the gender division of labor that kept women unequal to men.

The growing number of welfare rights groups began to link up in 1986 when Advocacy for Resources for Modern Survival (ARMS), a welfare rights group at the University of Massachusetts in Boston, started *Survival News*, a newspaper written for, about, and by low-income people. Still publishing in 1999, *Survival News* disseminates news about welfare rights issues in Massachusetts and in the U.S. to subscribers nationwide. A Milwaukee welfare mom's group called the Welfare Warriors began to publish *Welfare Mother's Voice*, a quarterly newspaper written for, about, and by welfare mothers in the mid-1980s. It too has survived.

On June 30, 1987, the 21st anniversary of the NWRO's founding, welfare mothers and organizers formed the National Welfare Rights Union (NWRU). With the 1988 Family Support Act (FSA) on the horizon, the NWRU "rededicated [itself] to the pursuit of social justice for all members of our society, particularly those who have been excluded from the benefits of this nation."[41] With leadership from the earlier movement and ties to other poor-people's groups, its first annual convention, in September 1988, drew more than 100 people from 18 states. In July 1989, the year the Family Support Act became effective, more than 350 people attended a National Survival Summit in Philadelphia organized by the NRWU, the National Union of the Homeless, and the National Anti-Hunger Coalition. The participants agreed to organize state survival summits and a national Up and Out of Poverty, Now! Campaign led by poor people. In October 1989, 120 participants from Illinois, Missouri, Michigan, Iowa Wisconsin, Indiana, Kentucky, Minnesota, South Dakota, and California convened in Chicago to develop common strategies. In subsequent years, survival summits targeted youth, hunger, homelessness, poor women, media blackouts of poor people's activism, and the negative fallout of the FSA. Rarely covered by the media and often invisible to anyone beyond the participants, the attack on welfare in the 1980s nonetheless brought more and more people, including many more poor women, into welfare rights activism.

The 1990s: During the 1990s, the NWRU, its affiliates, and a growing number of independent welfare rights groups actively opposed President Clinton's 1994 welfare reform bill, the January 1995 Republican Contract With America, and the 1996 Personal Responsibility Act. Their four-part strategy included organizing, legislative reform, legal challenges, and stepped-up public relations. All of the groups consisted mostly of women, but some of them dealt with women's issues more directly than others. The welfare rights agenda aimed to defeat a host of specific welfare policies that harmed or degraded poor women including workfare, fingerprinting, and the encroaching federal welfare reform law. Increasing numbers of groups, however, began to frame their resistance in gender terms. They highlighted their work as mothers; reminded the public that AFDC served children; stressed that some poor women, like some affluent women, needed or preferred to stay home with their children; maintained that working mothers needed quality, affordable childcare services; and insisted that battered women required special protections. A 1994 Survival News article written by two women on welfare stated: "The problem is poverty and devaluation of work of care, not welfare dependency."[42] Their call for adequate welfare benefits in the short run and a guaranteed annual income (for all) in the long run sought to validate this all important work. They also argued that like all women trying to balance caretaking and paid work, women on welfare needed a living wage, good benefits, and affordable childcare. Testifying before a 1994 Congressional Committee, NWRU President Marion Kramer stated: "All women who want to work outside the home should have the opportunity to earn a wage that will allow them to meet all the needs of their families. We also respect the right of all women who choose to stay in the home and nurture their children. They should be fully supported in their task for the important contribution that they are making to society." [43]

Taking up these women's issues, in the mid-1990s, JEDI for Women began to hold annual Mama Jams to celebrate low-income mothers, grandmothers, and nurturers whose work raising children our society often overlooks. The group's "10 Ways to Honor Mother and Nurturers," called for counting housework and family care as "work" and tax breaks for companies that offer childcare, health care, and flex-time benefits.[44] In 1995, some 30 JEDI families camped out at the Utah state capital to demand childcare.[45] A poster carried by a woman at a 1995 Boston demonstration declared that " workfare is mother mugging."[46] The burdens and celebrations of motherhood along with stories about local "movers and shakers" regularly filled the pages of both *Survival News* and the Welfare Mother's Voice.

The nineties also brought more active networking by welfare rights groups. In 1992, the Oakland-based WEAP gathered more than 400 poor women for the first Poor Women's Convention.[47] Their theme, "Under Attack, But Fighting Back" inspired the title of this book. On Valentine's Day, 1995, JEDI for Women mobilized groups in 77 cities and 38 states for a national day of action. The groups held simultaneous local demonstrations and sent legislators thousands of postcards which stated: " Our children's hearts are in your hands." In addition, the NWRU and other welfare rights groups again reached out to middle-class women's organizations with better, if limited, results than in the past. In the early 1990s, NOW renewed its fight against welfare reform and joined NWRU's Up and Out of Poverty, Now! Campaign. In 1993, NOW invited NWRU President Marian Kramer to address its annual convention, hired a former NWRO leader as an organizer, urged its local branches to work with poor women's organizations, and refused to endorse any political candidate who supported welfare reform. Together with Marion Kramer, NOW President Patricia Ireland was arrested trying to enter a congressional welfare hearing.[48] NOW also campaigned against the Contract with America and at its April 1995 rally identified welfare policy as another form of violence against women.

In 1994 and 1995, as the drive for welfare reform gained momentum and became more punitive, other feminist groups—less exclusively focused than before on challenging the gender division of labor—joined the battle in varying degrees. The NOW Legal Defense and Education Fund (which is not part of NOW) brought welfare mothers, anti-poverty advocates, and feminists into the same room for strategy talks. It also helped to organize eighty feminist, reproductive rights, religious, and right-to-life groups into a coalition that opposed any welfare measure that denied aid to children born while their mothers were on welfare. The Institute for Women's Policy Research, Wider Opportunities for Women, the Center for Reproductive Law and Policy, the National Black Women's Health Project, and the American Civil Liberties Union Reproductive Rights Project, among others, conducted research that helped to refute the popular myths that welfare undermined work and family ethics.

Women academics and professionals also tried to mobilize public opposition to welfare reform. In 1994, some 750 women academics supported ads in the *New York Review of Books*, and the *New Republic* that opposed President Clinton's welfare reform plan. The Committee of One Hundred Women, composed of prominent women artists, authors, professionals, academics, and trade unionists placed another ad in the *New York Times*, which declared: "A War Against Poor Women Is a War Against All Women!" The Committee also organized press conferences, lobbied Congress, and held a dramatic vigil outside the White House on Mother's Day. The Council of Presidents (of national women's organizations) representing six million women and ninety women's organizations developed a Women's Pledge on Welfare Reform to elicit opposition to welfare reform among feminist professional and advocacy groups. They also used their access to high level government officials to lobby against the law.

The efforts by welfare rights activists, advocacy groups, and women's organizations helped to stave off some of the worst reforms at the state and city level, and even won a few positive changes. But, in the end, all the opponents of welfare reform lost out to the political forces that eventually led Congress to pass the Personal Responsibility and Work Opportunity Reconciliation Act of 1996. Despite a terrible sense of defeat and the great hardship experienced by women on welfare since that time, welfare rights activism has not subsided. Indeed, the fourth edition of the Directory of Low Income Organizations Working on Welfare Issues published in April 1999 by the Welfare Law Center in New York City listed 189 groups in forty-four states and six groups in Canada.[49]

THE STRUGGLE CONTINUES: POST-TANF WELFARE ACTIVISM

WITH THE PASSAGE OF THE PERSONAL RESPONSIBILITY and Work Opportunity Act in 1996, the welfare rights groups and their allies entered a new ballgame. The welfare "reform" law converted AFDC into block grants, administered by the states, called TANF—now instead of dealing with one federal agency, welfare activists had to mount battles in fifty states. TANF also attempted to regulate women's work and family behavior by, among many things, imposing a five year lifetime limit on welfare eligibility; adding new, stricter work requirements; denying aid to children born while their mothers were on welfare; and limiting educational options for women on welfare.

Nonetheless, welfare rights activism has continued to grow. As the adverse impact of welfare reform has spread, groups in cities and towns across the nation have repeatedly mobilized large numbers of people to stem the tide. Four main strategies have evolved in this fight—damage control, service provision, litigation, and organizing.

In an effort to limit the damage and regain lost ground, most groups have felt compelled to lobby state and local lawmakers.

Prior to the implementation of TANF, activists protested ongoing welfare cuts and tried to influence the welfare reform plan submitted by their state to the federal government.[50] After 1997, in state after state, groups mustered the energy to lobby and rally, against the odds, for legislative corrections to ease the pain. They called for, and in some cases won, clearer standards for cutting people off welfare, reduced sanctions for violation of minor rules, waivers from the usual time limits and work requirements for battered women and persons with disabilities. The groups also fought for the acceptance of education as "community service work," a reversal of cuts to immigrant's benefits, employee protections for workfare participants, enforcement of federal sex discrimination laws in work and training programs, childcare for women leaving welfare, and no time limits for some recipients with earned income.

As welfare reform took its toll, damage control efforts expanded to include providing legal, social, childcare, and other services for people in desperate need, and gaining representation of women on welfare on the boards and commissions of mainstream institutions. Welfare groups also worked with anti-poverty lawyers—who have always supported the struggle for welfare rights[51]—to once again undo punitive welfare policies via the courts. The initial legal challenges targeted workfare abuses (such as nature of assignments, exemptions and worker protections) and state discrimination against new residents—with significant victories in both areas. Many states limited workfare abuses. And in May 1999, the U.S. Supreme Court ruled 7 to 2 that the states may not pay lower benefits to new residents because this practice violated the constitutional right to travel. The victory carried special meaning for mothers and their children fleeing male violence. The litigation by anti-poverty lawyers focused on specific sections of the new welfare reforms: child exclusion, child support cooperation, the elimination of the child support pass through, and a host of procedural measures. Some attorneys also tied their work to local organizing, especially around workfare cases that depended heavily on testimony by recipients and the involvement of community organizations.[52] Along with legislative victories, the successful court cases demonstrate the indifference to law and humanity among the architects of welfare reform.

While essential in the short run, the damage-control strategy also raised concerns. One advocate asked: "should legislation be a means to an end, that is part of a larger strategy to educate the public about the impact of welfare reform on workers, recipients, and poor communities."[53] Others feared that damage control might simply patch up and perhaps perpetuate an essentially harmful program. They wondered if they had made a pact with the devil! While the focus on social service and individual advocacy helped many people, still other observers worried that this strategy drained the limited resources of the advocacy groups. The litigation strategy made important gains, but oftentimes seemed far away from the daily struggle.

The stratagy of organizing and building a poor people's movement focused on wider social change. The multitude of organizing drives by local welfare groups cannot be recounted here. However, the work of two organizations—the Kensington Welfare Rights Union (KWRU), a chapter of the NWRU, and the Association of Community Organizations for Reform Now, or ACORN—captures the spirit and intent of this strategy and reveals some of its dilemmas.

The Kensington Welfare Rights Union (KWRU) describes itself as an "organization of the poor committed to speaking for themselves and organizing to build a social movement to end poverty and human right violations."[54] For years this multiracial organization of women and men has conducted militant actions at welfare offices in Philadelphia and has taken-over numerous abandoned housing units. In June 1997, KWRU launched a Poor People's Economic Human Rights Campaign. It included a ten-day March For Our Lives from Philadelphia's Liberty Bell to the United Nations in New York City. The following June, KWRU organized the New Freedom Bus, which traveled to 35 urban and rural communities across the country in a month and regularly won local media coverage. This trip ended on July 1,1998, with a National Tribunal at the Church of the United Nations, where the marchers presented the stories of human rights violations they had gathered along the way.

In October 1999, the Economic Human Rights Campaign, which now claims over 35 organizational members, conducted its third month-long march of poor and homeless families, this time linked to international struggles. The March of the Americas: Continuing the March for Our Lives traveled from Washington, D.C. to the UN. The marchers again camped along the road, held press conferences, met with community activists, and supported local protests. KWRU billed the action as "the focal point for the efforts going on around the country where people are organizing for their survival needs?"[55]

ACORN, a twenty-year old organization, describes itself as a national network of community groups that now links welfare to work issues. With chapters in many cities, ACORN became a player in efforts to "unionize" workfare participants, winning especially large drives in New York and Los Angeles. ACORN has also begun to monitor the $3 billion in federal money allotted to the states for welfare-to-work programs. It plans to see that the states use the funds to create new jobs and to ensure that they involve community groups in the planning. Finally, ACORN, whose July 1998 National Organizers Summit on Welfare Reform in Milwaukee, Wisconsin, drew more than 1500 people representing more than 30 organizations, has joined with the AFL-CIO and others to win city ordinances requiring that firms receiving city contracts or tax breaks pay their employees a living wage, or what a full-time, year-round worker needs to keep a family of four out of poverty. [56]

Welfare groups have coordinated their efforts in still other ways. Regional groups have sprung up, especially in the Northwestern states, where many welfare rights and advocacy groups—led by women—exist. In August 1998, more than seventy-five welfare activists, from twenty-three organizations in twelve western states, attended the Western Region Activist's Summit in Portland, Oregon. Seeking to develop a collective response to welfare reform, they planned a joint protest for the next anniversary of the federal welfare bill.[57]

In October 1998, more than 400 poor and homeless people from across the nation attended the Poor People's Summit in Philadelphia, sponsored by the KWRU, the National Union of Hospital and Health Care Employees, and Temple University of School of Social Work as part of KWRU's ongoing effort to build a Poor People's Movement. In December 1998, Jobs for Justice, an activist organization made up of sixty unions and community groups, rallied thousands of people in over sixty cities for a national day of action for jobs and against welfare reform. The first coordinated national protest since TANF, it received considerable media attention. In May, 1999, the welfare rights community rallied again, calling for a national moratorium on time limits for welfare benefits. Called by the People's Network for a New Safety Net and endorsed by many other groups, the action began on May 1, to honor the historic workers' holiday, and ended on Mothers Day, May 10, to recognize women's unpaid work in the home.[58] In August, 1999, recipients in twenty-five states rallied to "stop the clock that is ticking away for millions of other poor people facing federally mandated expiration of benefits in the year 2003." To dramatize their demand, more than one-hundred Los Angeles welfare recipients threw down fistfulls of wrist watches and stomped on them until they cracked. They also presented two-thousand watches to their senator, Barbara Boxer, who has been sympathetic to their concerns.[59]

New Alliances: The widespread impact of TANF has brought welfare rights groups together with constituencies that previously ignored them, including feminist organizations, immigrant rights groups, trade unions, and religious institutions. Because of a lack of national media coverage of their rallies, press conferences, and other welfare rights actions, the wider public remains largely unaware of the new alliances.

Few know that some feminist groups fought against the passage of the 1996 welfare law. Since then some feminist organizations have tried (so far unsuccessfully) to challenge the child exclusion portion of welfare reform in the courts, worked to ensure that states exempted battered women from work requirements as mandated by the law, and fought against employment discrimination in welfare-to-work programs. Immigrant rights groups rallied their ranks because TANF denied welfare, Food Stamps, and SSI benefits to many immigrants. Organized labor has also joined the struggle, because welfare reform's work rules threaten to flood the labor market with tens of thousands of recipients which could result in lower union wages and fewer union jobs.

These collaborations have effectively enlarged the welfare reform opposition and brought more visibility to the issue. However, they have also raised some new concerns. First, the greater public sympathy for immigrants, paid workers, and battered women threatens to divide so-called "deserving" from "undeserving" recipients. The groups representing the more "popular" poor have already reversed some welfare provisions that harm their members most. The traditional welfare rights activists hope that their new allies will support the rights of all women on welfare and stick with the issue for the long haul. The increased involvement of professional advocates also risks diminishing the leadership role of poor women on welfare—a historical point of contention in the welfare rights and most other cross-class movements.

Finally, poor women may be having a harder time keeping their women's issues on the agenda, especially mothering, childcare, pay equity, and male violence. Indeed, TANF's emphasis on work requirements and the expansion of workfare has focused attention on paid work, low wages, and the working poor. The labor unions and large community-based organizations, often led by male organizers, stand behind worker's rights. They organize workfare participants, campaign for a livable wage, and lobby for jobs. Poor women actively support these important labor market goals. But they still have to remind their allies that, as women, they need the option of choosing when paid work is best for them and their families and when it is not. They point out that since mothers already work in the home or in part-time paid jobs, women need income as much, if not more than they need work. Therefore, many welfare rights groups led by women demand some kind of guaranteed income in addition to jobs at a living wage (with pay equity and childcare). They also believe that all workers should have the right to claim welfare without stigma, when their family circumstances demand it.[60] I would add that the welfare rights movement might also pay more explicit attention to racial discrimination in both work and welfare policies.

New Tools: During the 1990s, access to the Internet has greatly enhanced efforts of welfare rights groups to communicate and organize. In 1998, the loose welfare rights network became electronically linked through a project funded by foundations and managed by the Welfare Law Center in New York City. The Low Income Networking and Communications (LINC) project provides technical assistance, posts the newsletters of numerous organizations on its web site, and operates an email list for welfare activists. This electronic exchange makes it possible for activists to share information about local actions, policy developments, analytic critiques, and future strategies. It also allows groups too poor to send members to meetings in other states to stay in touch with one another and has sparked various collaborative actions ranging from conferences to national protests.

Besides the Internet, welfare advocates have turned research into an advocacy tool. Some have concluded that without hard data on the impact of welfare reform, it would be difficult to dispute those heralding its success. In the mid-1990s, the Unitarian Universalist Service Committee initiated the National Welfare Monitoring and Advocacy Project which urged recipient groups, researchers, and service providers to use a common survey to monitor the implementation of welfare reform as a human rights violation. By December 1998, some twenty national and local organization joined this effort as partners.[61] In addition, numerous

Members of the Kensington Welfare Rights Union in Philadelphia protest against human service proposals, 1995. [Harvey Finkel/Impact Visuals]

foundations, universities, think tanks, advocacy organizations, and even some state governments have began to count and in some instances to track the women who left welfare. The data from these various sources has documented the sharp drop in the welfare rolls. At the same time it has confirmed the stress and hardship that women on welfare have recounted to the media, at public hearings, and elsewhere. When TANF comes up for renewal in the year 2002, advocates plan to use this data to convince Congress that welfare reform has not worked.

Policy Alternatives. The expiration of TANF also provides the opportunity to think about more constructive alternatives. The proposals that seek to improve welfare in the short run try to respond to what their backers believe today's conservative political

149

climate might tolerate. Other advocates take a longer-range view and seek a cash assistance program that might increase women's economic autonomy as well as provide more jobs and better wages.

Rewards States For Positive Policies The NOW Legal Defense and Education Fund and other groups have developed legislation to reward states for developing welfare programs which address women's poverty, rather than simply reduce the rolls. The proposed Bonus for Building Real Opportunities for Poor Families, referrd to as BOB, provides a total of $1 billion in bonuses over five years to ten states whose welfare programs most effectively redress inadequate childcare, insufficient job training, and domestic violence. Congress failed to act on the bill when a few legislators introduced it the House and the Senate. But plans exist to have it reintroduced.[62]

Positive Work Incentives In 1996, the co-chairs of the Economists' Policy Group for Women's Issues proposed the Help for Working Parents (HWP) program, which stressed work as the means to women's economic independence. HWP proposed to supplement minimum wage jobs with non-cash benefits such as childcare, health care, and housing assistance and to expand the Earned Income Tax Credit. While costly, the authors argued that this program would help move poor parents out of poverty regardless of a woman's marital status.[63]

Job Creation and Living Wage. Many groups have begun to fight for more jobs at a livable wage. Despite low unemployment in some parts of the country, in large cities where most recipients live, the jobless rates remain high. The living wage drives have had considerable success in many cities and have become the base for organizing the working poor.

In addition to thinking about what is possible today, it is also useful to invent alternatives, even if at first they at first seem unrealistic or outrageous. The following proposals focus on enhancing the autonomy of women in the labor market and in the home. They try to come to terms with a future in which there may not be paid work or an adequate income for everyone, but one in which people will still need a decent standard of living and will still depend on carework in the home.

Breadwinner and Caretaker Parity for Women moves beyond the constraints of the political climate to a more visionary stance. Developed by Nancy Fraser, a professor of political philosophy, it allows women to choose between home and market work by making both sites more women-friendly. Breadwinner parity for women involves: the creation of permanent, fulltime, high paying jobs for women; the development of more childcare, elder care, and other services that help women balance work and home; the elimination of labor market barriers such as unequal pay, occupational segregation, sex discrimination, and sexual harassment; and social insurance plans that account for women's labor market needs. Caregiver parity for women includes a generous caregiver's allowance to compensate women's work in child bearing, child raising, housework, and other caretaking activities that serve families and wider society. For those unable to do either waged or carework, Fraser added a need-based, means-tested benefit instead of wages or government allowance.[64]

Ann Orloff, a professor of sociology at the University of Wisconsin has developed a more radical reform that targets the underlying gender relations of power.[65] Orloff argues for greater autonomy for women by which she means the capacity to form and maintain households without having to marry. Therefore, Orloff calls for programs that ensure women access to independent incomes. Only this, she holds, will insulate women from labor market poverty and free them from economic dependence on men and marriage. With an independent income (such as generous welfare benefits or a guaranteed income) women can escape both market exploitation and male domination. Martha Fineman, a professor at Columbia University School of Law goes one step further. She calls for an end to the legal basis of marriage (not necessarily the relationship itself), the elimination of all government subsidies and protections designed to uphold this institution, and the recognition that nurturing units, i.e. caregiving families whatever their shape or structure are inevitability dependent and may require some type of government support.[66]

Whether or not you agree with these particular proposals, the important point remains that only by thinking outside the box can the supporters of women, welfare rights and a more just society begin to put the public policy agenda back on track. The Right never fears making outrageous proposals, and many of their ideas deemed realistic at first, have become law, including ending welfare and eliminating entitlements. Progressive social change requires both pressure from below and a willingness to take risks. In the words of Frederick Douglass, abolitionist and supporter of women's rights, " If there is no Struggle, there is not progress. . . . Power concedes nothing without a demand." And as the women activists have always known, we must dare to struggle if we expect to win!

NOTES

Part 1: Still Under Attack: Women and Welfare Reform

1. Bill Clinton and Al Gore, *Putting People First: How We Can All Change America*, cited in "Charge to the Working Group on Welfare Reform, Family Support and Independence." This group, chaired by David Ellwood and Bruce Reed, was formed by President Clinton in June 1993 to develop his welfare reform plan.
2. Katha Pollitt, *The Nation*, April 13, 1998.
3. Legal Services of New Jersey, *Assessing Work First: What Happens After Welfare?* (New Brunswick, NJ, June 1999), P.74.
4. Samuel Bowles, "The Crisis of Liberal Democratic Capitalism," *Politics and Society* 11 (1982), pp. 51–93; Samuel Bowles, David Gordon, Thomas Wieisskopf, *Beyond the Wasteland: A Democratic Alternative to Economic Decline* (Garden City, NJ: Anchor/Doubleday, 1983); Samuel Bowles, David Gordon, Thomas Wieisskopf, "Power and Profits: The Social Structure of Accumulation and the Profitability of the Post-War U.S. Economy." *Review of Radical Economics* 1&2 (1986), pp. 32–167. Fred Block, "Rethinking the Political Economy of the Welfare State," in F. Block, R.A. Cloward, B. Ehrenreich, and F.F. Piven (eds) *The Mean Season: the Attack on the Welfare State* (New York: Pantheon, 1987), pp. 109–160.
5. U.S. Congressional Budget Office, *Reducing Entitlement Spending* (Washington, D.C.: U.S. Government Printing Office, 1994), Table 1, p. x.
6. The American Enterprise Institute, *A Community of Self-Reliance: A New Consensus on Family and Welfare* (Washington, D.C.: American Enterprise Institute, 1987), p. 4.

7. Robert Rector, "Combatting Family Disintegration, Crime and Dependence: Welfare Reform and Beyond," *Heritage Foundation Backgrounder*, April 8, 1994, p. 7.

8. White House Working Group on the Family, *The Family: Preserving America's Future*, Press Release and Report, (U.S. Department of Education, Office of the Under Secretary, November 13, 1986), p. 21; Michael Tanner, "Ending Welfare As We Know It," *Policy Analysis* 212 (July 7, 1994), pp. 22–23; Charles Murray, "The Emerging White Underclass and How To Save It," *Philadelphia Inquirer*, November 15, 1993, p. A15.

9. U.S. House of Representatives, Committee on Ways and Means, *Overview of Entitlement Programs, 1998 Green Book* (Washington, D.C.: U.S. Government Printing Office, 1998), T. 7–19, p. 440.

10. Martin Gilens, "Racial Attitudes and Opposition to Welfare," *Journal of Politics* 57 (4), pp. 4994–1014; *Los Angeles Times Poll, no. 96*, April 1985; K. Sue Jewell, *From Mammy to Miss America and Beyond: Cultural Images & The Shaping of U.S. Social Policy* (New York: Routledge).

11. Jason DeParle, "Shrinking Welfare Rolls Leave Record High Share of Minorities," *New York Times*, July 27, 1998.

12. See, for example, Paul M. Sweezy, *The Theory of Capitalist Development* (New York: Monthly Review Press, 1968), pp. 239–253.

13. See, for example, Gosta Epsing-Anderson, *Three Worlds of Welfare Capitalism* (Princeton, NJ: Princeton University Press, 1990); Gosta Epsing-Anderson, *Politics Against Markets: The Social Democratic Road To Power* (Princeton, NJ: Princeton University Press, 1985); Frances Fox Piven and Richard A. Cloward, *The New Class War: Reagan's Attack on the Welfare State and its Consequences* (New York: Pantheon Books, 1982), p. 118.

14. U.S. House of Representatives, Committee on Ways and Means, *Overview of Entitlement Programs, 1998 Green Book* (Washington, D.C.: U.S. Government Printing Office, 1998), T. 7–2, p. 402.

15. U.S. House of Representatives, Committee on Ways and Means, *Overview of Entitlement Programs, 1998 Green Book* (Washington, D.C.: U.S. Government Printing Office, 1998), T. 6, p. 413; U.S. Congress, Congressional Budget Office, *The Economic and Budget Outlook, 2000–2009* (Washington D.C.: U.S. Government Printing Office, 1999), Historical Tables, p. 136; Robert Pear, "Welfare and Food Stamp Rolls End Six Years of Increases," *New York Times*, March 14, 1995, p. 18; Center For Law and Social Policy, "AFDC Caseload Declines: Implications for Block Grant Planning" (Washington, D.C.: October 2, 1995), Factsheet, p. 1.

16. Labor Institute, *Corporate Power and the American Dream* (New York: Labor Institute, April 1995), p. 82.

17. Francis Piven & Richard Cloward, *Regulating The Poor: The Functions of*

Public Assistance (New York: Pantheon, 1971).

18. U.S. House of Representatives, Committee on *Ways and Means, Overview of Entitlement Programs, 1998 Green Book* (Washington, D.C.: U.S. Government Printing Office, 1998), T. 6, p. 413.

19. U.S. Department of Health and Human Services, Administration For Children and Families, *Aid to Families With Dependent Children/Temporary Aid To Needy Families, 1960–1998* (April 1999). [http://www.acf.dhhs.gov.]

20. U.S. Department of Health and Human Services, Administration For Children and Families, *Aid to Families With Dependent Children/Temporary Aid To Needy Families,1960–1998* (April 1999). [http://www.acf.dhhs.gov.]

21. "The Job Centers: An HRA Initiative," Information Sheet, Community Food Research Center, (New York: no date).

22. Irene Bush and M. Katherine Kraft, *Women on Welfare: What They Have To Say About Becoming Self-Sufficient* (New Jersey Department of Human Services, Office of Policy and Planning, April 1997).

23. Legal Services of New Jersey, *Assessing Work First: What Happens After Welfare?* (New Brunswick, NJ: June 1999), p. 75.

24. Barbara Vobejda and Judith Herman, "Sanctions Fuel Drop in Welfare Rolls,"*Washington Post*, March 23, 1998, p. A1.

25. State News, *Clasp Update*, July 31, 1999, p. 8.

26. Aaron Bernstein, "Where The Jobs Are The Skills Aren't,"*Business Week*, September 19, 1988, p.108; U.S. Department of Labor, *WorkForce 2000: Work and Workers for the 21st Century* (Washington, D.C.: U.S. Government Printing Office, 1987).

27. National Alliance of Business, *Employment Policies: Looking To The Year 2000,* February 1986, p.I,8.

28. National Alliance of Business, *Employment Policies: Looking To The Year 2000,* February 1986, p.I,8.

29. Fodice quoted in Kevin Sack, "In Mississippi, Will Poor Grow Poorer With State Welfare Plan," *New York Times*, October 23, 1995, p. A1; Lawrence M. Mead, *The New Politics of Poverty* (New York: Basic Books, 1992), p. 12; Center on Social Welfare Policy and Law, "Welfare Reform Hearings: January 1995" (Washington D.C.: February 8, 1995), p. 1, 441–442.

30. See for example, LaDonna Pavetti, "The Dynamics of Welfare and Work: Exploring the Process By Which Young Women Work Their Way Off Welfare,"cited in U.S. House, Committee on Ways and Means, *Overview of Entitlement Programs, 1994 Green Book,* (Washington, D.C.: U.S. Government Printing Office, 1994), pp.40, 43–44.

31. "Single Mothers, Jobs and Welfare: What The Data Tell Us,"*Research in Brief* (Washington, D.C.: Institute for Women's Policy Research, December 1997), p. 2; "Welfare To Work: The Job Opportunities of AFDC Recipients," *Research in Brief* (Washington, D.C.: Institute for Women's

Policy Research, March 1995); Roberta Spalter-Roth, Beverly Burr, Heidi Hartmann, and Lois Shaw, *Welfare That Works: The Working Lives of AFDC Recipients* (Washington D.C.: Institute for Women's Policy Research, March 20, 1995), pp. 40, 43–44.

32. Jan Hagen and Irene Lurie, *Implementing JOBS: Progress and Promise*, (Albany, NY: Nelson A. Rockefeller Institute of Government, State University of New York, 1994), p. 230; Robert Moffitt, *Incentive Effects of the U.S. Welfare System: A Review* (SR #48) (Madison, WI: Institute for Research on Poverty, University of Wisconsin-Madison, March 1991); Riccio, James & Friedlander, Daniel, *GAIN: Program Strategies, Participation, Patterns and First Year Impact in Six Counties* (New York: Manpower Demonstration Research Corporation, May 1992); U.S. Government Accounting Office, *Welfare To Work: States Begin JOBS, but Fiscal and Other Problems May Impede Their Progress* (Washington, D.C.: U. S. Government Printing Office, September 1992), p. 43.

33. Center on Social Welfare Policy and Law, Preliminary Analysis of Title I of HR 4, as passed by the Senate on September 9, 1995 (Washington, D.C.: September 26, 1995), pp. 5–6; Mark Greenberg, *Understanding the Clinton Welfare Bill: Two Years and Work* (Washington, D.C.: Center for Law and Social Policy, July 12), pp. 1–15.

34. *Linking The Neighborhoods*, Special Issues (Welfare Law Center, March 25, 1997), NP.

35. David Barstow, "A. T. M. Cards Fail To Live Up To Promises Made to the Poor," *New York Times*, August 16, 1999, p. A1.

36. Sharon Parrott, *Welfare Recipients Who Find Jobs: What Do We Know About Their Employment and Earnings?* (Washington, D.C.: Center on Budget and Policy Priorities, November 16, 1998), p. 9.

37. Nicholas Timmins, "Reform May Push U.S. Poor Into Squalor," *Financial Times*, November 23, 1998.

38. Sharon Parrott, *Welfare Recipients Who Find Jobs: What Do We Know About Their Employment and Earnings?* (Washington, D.C.: Center on Budget and Policy Priorities, November 16, 1998), pp. 5–19.

39. Children's Defense Fund and National Coalition for the Homeless, *Welfare To What?: Early Findings on Family Hardship and Well-Being* (Washington, D.C.: 1999).

40. Newsletter, Hunger Action Network of New York State, February 15, 1995, p. 8; Jonathan Rabinowitz, Welfare Fallout Traps Mothers: Plan Threatens Education, *New York Times*, May 19, 1995, p. B1; Irene Skricki, *Unheard Voices: Participants Evaluate the JOBS Program* (Washington, D.C.: Coalition on Human Needs, January 1993), p. 13.

41. Irene Skricki, *Unheard Voices: Participants Evaluate the JOBS Program* (Washington, D.C.: Coalition on Human Needs, January 1993), p. 13.

42. Jack Tweedie & Dana Reichert, "Tracking Recipients After They Leave Welfare," National Conference of State Legislatures Summaries of State Follow-up Studies.

43. Robert Kuttner, "The Boom In Poverty," *Boston Globe*, March 21, 1999, p. E07.

44. LaDonna Pavetti, *Learning From The Voices of Mothers: Single Mothers' Perceptions of the Trade-offs Between Welfare and Work*, (New York: Manpower Demonstration Research Corporation, January 1993), p. 8.

45. Ann Withorn & Pamela Jons, "Worrying About Welfare Reform: Community Based Agencies Respond: Summary Report" (Boston: Academic Working Group on Poverty, 1999), p. 5; CDF News Release, "Welfare To What?: Early Findings on Family Hardship and Well-Being"(Washington, DC: December 2, 1998); Randy Albeda, "What Welfare Reform Has Wrought," *Dollars & Sense*, January/February 1999, p. 17; Jason DeParle, "Wisconsin Welfare Overhaul Justified Hope and Some Fear," *New York Times*, January 15, 1999; "Impact of Welfare Reform on Homelessness," *Safety Network: The Newsletter of the National Coalition for the Homeless*, vol. 17, no. 2 (May–June 1998), p. 1, 4; Margaret A. Leonard, "We Need to Stand Together: The Impact of Welfare Reform on the Dudley Street Neighborhood and the Communities Response To the Challenge"(Roxbury, MA: February 1999), pp. 4–6.

46. Joyce Short, "The Great Enemy of Morality is Indifference," *Legal Service of New Jersey Report*, February/ March 1999, p. 9; CBPP on poverty (children living below one-half the poverty line) cited in CDF summary sheet.

47. Lisa Dodson and Paula Rayman, *Welfare in Transition* (Radicliff Public Policy Institute, 1998), p. 20.

48. *The Impact Of Welfare Reform In The 30 Largest U.S. Cities: 1999* (Washington, D.C.: Brookings Institution, February 1999).

49. Ann Withorn & Pamela Jons, *Worrying About Welfare Reform: Community Based Agencies Respond: Summary Report* (Boston: Academic Working Group on Poverty, 1999), p. 5.

50. Legal Services of New Jersey, *Assessing Work First: What Happens After Welfare?* (New Brunswick, NJ: June 1999), p. 74.

51. "State News," *CLASP UPDATE*, April 39, 1999; June 18, 1999; "Public Job Creation Initiatives," *CLASP UPDATE*, February 26, 1999, p. 8.

52. Jason Deparle, "Leftover Money For Welfare Baffles, or Inspires, States," *New York Times*, August 29, 1999, p. A1, 30, 31.

53. Mimi Abramovitz, *Regulating The Lives of Women: Social Welfare Policy From Colonial Times To The Present*, 2^{d} ed (Boston: South End Press, 1996).

54. David Popenoe, "The Family Transformed," *Family Affairs*, Summer/Fall 1989, vol. 2, no. 2–3 (Institute For American Affairs, Working Group on the Family), p. 1, 2.

55. *Personal Responsibility and Work Opportunity Reconciliation Act (PWORA): A Conference Report To Accompany H.R. 3734*, July 30, 1996, p. 9.

56. Stephanie Ventura, "Births to Unmarried Mothers: United States 1980–92," PHS 95-1931, Series 21 #53, (Washington, D.C.: U.S. Government Printing Office, 1995), p. 3. Stephanie Ventura, Joyce Martin, Sally Curtin, and T. J. Mathews, National Center Final Natality Statistics, 1996, vol. 46, no. 11 supplement. 100 pp. PHS 98-1120 (http://www.cdc.gov/nchswww); Sheryl Gay Stolberg, "Birth Rates at New Low as Teen Age Pregnancy Declines," *New York Times*, April 29, 1999, p. A26.

57. National Governors' Association Center for Best Practices, "Round Two Summary of Selected Elements of State Programs for Temporary Assistance for Needy Families," March 14, 1999 [http:// www.nga.org/CBP/Activities/WelfareReform.asp].

58. Because anti-abortion groups feared that the child exclusion provision would lead pregnant women to seek abortions, they insisted that the bonus be based on non-marital births *and* abortions as a percentage of births to all women in the state instead of just within the AFDC caseload, thus linking control of reproduction among AFDC women to control of all women in the state.

59. NOW Legal Defence and Education Fund (1999), *What the States Didn't Tell You: a State by State Guide to the Welfare Law's Reproductive Rights Agendam* (New York City; NLDEF), p. 1.

60. Timothy Egan, "Take This Bribe, Please For Values To Be Received," *New York Times*, November 12, 1995, p. E5.

61. "Health Education Groups Seek End of Abstinence Unless Married Fed Program"; "Clasp Resources On How States Can Use TANF Funds To Support Reproductive Health and Teen Parent Initiative," *CLASP UPDATE*, June 18, 1999, pp. 16–17.

62. Stuart Butler and Anna Kondratas, *Out of the Poverty Trap: A Conservative Strategy For Welfare Reform* (New York: Free Press, 1987), pp. 138–139; Charles Murray, "The Emerging White Underclass and How To Save It," *Philadelphia Inquirer*, November 15, 1993, p. A15.

63. U.S. House of Representatives, Committee on Ways and Means, *Overview of Entitlement Programs,1998 Green Book* (Washington, D.C.: U.S. Government Printing Office, 1998), T. 7–19, p. 440.

64. Data from the 1988 National Survey of Family Growth indicate that 88 percent of never-married women, 69 percent of previously married women, and 40 percent of the married women had unintended pregnancies. U.S. Department of Health and Human Services, *Report to Congress on Out-Of-Wedlock Childbearing* (Executive Summary) (West Hyattsville, MD: September 1995), p. 8.

65. Kristin A. Moore, "Reducing Out of Wed-Lock Births: What States Need to Know," *Child Trends*, March 1998.

66. The Annie C. Casey Foundation, *1999 Kids Count Data Book: State Profiles of Child Well Being* (Baltimore, 1999), p. 21.

67. Karen Judd, *Welfare Reform Update* (Portchester, NY: Pro Choice Resource Center, Inc, 10573, 1999), p. 6–7. (Citing study conducted by Rutgers University for the NJ Department of Human Services.) *Report on the Impact of New Jersey's Family Development Program: Result from a Pre-Post Analysis of AFDC Case Heads from 1990–1996.* (Cited in *Welfare News*, June 30, 1998, p. 8.)

68. Nina Bernstein, "Foster Care System Wary of Welfare Cuts," *New York Times*, November 19, 1995, p. 1, 26.

69. Robert Rector, "Combating Family Disintegration, Crime, Dependence: Welfare Reform and Beyond," *Heritage Foundation Backgrounder*, April 8, 1994, p. 10.

70. U. S. House of Representatives, Select Committee on Children, Youth, and Families, *Safety Net Programs: Are They Reaching Poor Children*, Report 99-1023, 99th Cong; 2d session (Washington D. C.: U.S. Government Printing Office, December 1986), p. 333.

71. Ann Withorn, *Not For Lack of Trying: The Struggle Over Welfare Reform in Massachusetts 1992–1998* (Boston: John W. McCormack Institute For Public Affairs, March 1999), p. 6.

72. U.S. Bureau of the Census, *Household and Family Characteristics, March 1997*, Current Population Reports, Series P-20, no. 509 (Washington, D.C.: U.S. Government Printing Office, April 1998), p. 4.

73. Heather Mac Donald, "The Real Welfare Problem is Illegitimacy," *City Journal* (http: www.city-journal.org/html/8_laL/htm), p. 14.

74. Myron Magnet, "Problem No 1: The Children," *New York Times*, November 25, 1994, p. A37. Healther Mac Donald, "The Real Welfare Problem is Illegitimacy," *City Journal* (http: www.city-journal.org/html/8_laL/htm), p.14.

75. David Lond, Robert Wood, and Hilary Kopp, *The Effects of LEAP and Enhanced Services in Cleveland: Ohios Learning, Earning, and Parenting Programs for Teenage Parents on Welfare* (New York: Manpower Demonstration Research Corporation, October 1994), p. vi.

76. Karen Judd, *Welfare Reform Update* (Portchester, NY: Pro Choice Resource Center, Inc., 10573, 1999), pp. 6–22.

77. La Donna, Pavetti, *Learning From The Voices of Mothers: Single Mothers' Perceptions of the Trade-offs Between Welfare and Work,* (New York: Manpower Demonstration Research Corporation, January 1993), p. 21.

78. Ruth Coniff, Big Bad Welfare, *The Progressive*, August 24, p. 21.

79. "Snapshot of America's Families," Urban Institute, cited in *CLASP UPDATE*, February 26, 1999, pp.12–13. (See also www.urban.org.)

80. Legal Services of New Jersey, *Assessing Work First: What Happens After Welfare?* (New Brunswick, NJ: June 1999), p. 78.

81. Mimi Abramovitz, *Regulating The Lives of Women: Social Welfare Programs From Colonial Times To The Present*, 2d ed. (Boston: South End Press, 1996).

82. Center on Budget and Policy Priorities, "Summary of Effects of House Bill H.R.4 on Low Income Programs," (Washington, D.C.:1995, short brief), p. 3.

83. Editors, "Supreme Mischief," *New York Times*, June 24, 1999, p. A26; Linda Greenhouse, "States Are Given New Legal Shield By Supreme Court," *New York Times*, June 24, 1999, p. A1, A22.

Part 2: A Program Just for Single Mothers

1. Stephanie Coontz, *The Social Origins of Private Life: A History of American Families, 1600–1900* (London: Verso, 1989), p. 167.

2. Mary Ryan, *Womanhood in America, from Colonial Times to the Present* (New York: New Viewpoints, 1975), pp. 100–101.

3. Benjamin Klebaner, "Poverty and Its Relief in American Thought, 1815–61," in Compassion and Responsibility: *Readings in the History of Social Welfare Policy in the United States*, ed. Frank R. Breul and Steven J. Diner (Chicago: University of Chicago Press, 1980), p. 123l.

4. Stephanie Coontz, *Social Origins of Private Life*, pp. 161–209.

5. Walter I. Trattner, *From Poor Law to Welfare State: A History of Social Welfare in America*, 4th ed. (New York: Free Press, 1989), p. 53.

6. Michael B. Katz, *In the Shadow of the Poorhouse: A Social History of Welfare in America* (New York: Basic Books, 1986), p. 23.

7. David Rothman, *The Discovery of Asylum: Social Order and Disorder in the New Republic* (Boston: Little, Brown and Co., 1971), p. 183; Walter I. Trattner, *From Poor Law to Welfare State*, pp. 55–56; Michael B. Katz, *In the Shadow of the Poorhouse*, pp. 37–42.

8. June Axinn and Herman Levin, *Social Welfare: A History of the American Response to Need* (New York: Harper and Row, 1975), p. 100.

9. Blanche Coll, *Perspectives in Public Welfare: A History* (Washington, D.C.: Department of Health, Education and Welfare, Office of Research, Demonstration and Training, 1969, Monograph), p. 43.

10. Michael B. Katz, *In the Shadow of the Poorhouse*, p. 37, Table 2.1.

11. Pricilla Ferguson Clement, "Nineteenth Century Welfare Policy, Programs and Poor Women: Philadelphia as a Case Study, *Feminist Studies* 1 (Spring 1992) 35–58 (p. 45, Table 5).

12. Blanche Coll, *Perspectives in Public Welfare*, p. 58.

13. David M. Schneider and Albert Deutch, *The History of Public Welfare in*

New York State, 1867–1940 (Chicago: University of Chicago Press, 1951), p. 38.

14. Joseph Rayback, *A History of American Labor* (New York: Free Press, 1960), p. 159.

15. David Gordon, Richard Edwards, and Michael Reich, *Segmented Work, Divided Workers: The Historical Transformation of Labor in the United States* (Cambridge and London: Cambridge University Press, 1982), pp. 56–100.

16. Christine Stansell, *City of Women: Sex and Class in New York 1789–1860* (Urbana: University of Illinois Press, 1987), pp. 63–75.

17. Michael B. Katz, *In the Shadow of the Poorhouse*, p. 108.

18. Lela Costin, "Cruelty to Children: A Dormant Issue and Rediscovery 1920–1960," *Social Service Review* 66, No. 2 (June 1992): 179.

19. Blanche Coll, *Perspectives in Public Welfare*, p. 68.

20. Unless otherwise indicated, the discussion of Mothers' Pensions draws on Mimi Abramovitz, *Regulating the Lives of Women: Social Welfare Policy from Colonial Times to the Present* (Boston: South End Press, 1988); Linda Gordon, *Pitied but Not Entitled: Single Mothers and the History of Welfare* (New York: Free Press, 1994); Mark H. Leff, "The Mothers' Pension Movement in the Progressive Era," in *Compassion and Responsibility*, ed. Frank R. Breul and Steven J. Diner, p. 247; and Gwendolyn Mink, *The Wages of Motherhood: Inequality in the Welfare State, 1917–1942* (Ithaca, NY: Cornell University Press, 1995).

21. Unless otherwise indicated, the discussion of ADC draws on Mimi Abramovitz, *Regulating the Lives of Women*; Eveline M. Burns, *The American Social Security System* (New York: Houghton Mifflin Co., 1949), p. 362; Linda Gordon, *Pitied but Not Entitled*; Gwendolyn Mink, *The Wages of Motherhood*; and James Patterson, *America's Struggle Against Poverty 1900–1980* (Cambridge: Harvard University Press, 1981).

22. Jerry Cates, *Insuring Inequality: Administrative Leadership in Social Security, 1935–1954* (Ann Arbor, MI: University of Michigan Press, 1983).

23. Gwendolyn Mink, "Why Should Poor Single Mothers Have to Work Outside the Home?" (unpub. ms., 1995), p. 10.

24. U.S. Congress, Joint Economic Committee, Subcommittee on Fiscal Policy, *Studies in Public Welfare, Paper No. 20, Handbook of Public Income Transfer Programs, 1975* (Washington, D.C.: Government Printing Office, 1974), pp. 169–70, Tables 9 and 10.

25. James Patterson, *America's Struggle Against Poverty*, p. 78.

26. U.S. Congress, House Committee on Ways and Means, *Overview of Entitlement Programs, 1993 Green Book* (Washington, D.C.: Government Printing Office, 1993), p. 1313, Table 4.

27. Donald Bartlett and James B. Steele, America: *Who Really Pays the Taxes?*

(New York: Simon and Schuster, 1994), pp. 68–69.

28. James Patterson, *America's Struggle Against Poverty,* pp. 89–90; Lucy Komisar, *Down and Out in the USA: A History of Social Welfare* (New York: New Viewpoints, 1974), pp. 72–73.

29. Susan Hartmann, *The Home Front and Beyond: American Women in the 1940s* (Boston: Twayne Publishers, 1982), p. 90.

30. Steven Mintz and Susan Kellog, *Domestic Revolutions: A Social History of American Family Life* (New York: Free Press, 1988), p. 161.

31. Alice Kessler-Harris, *Out to Work: A History of Wage Earning Women in the United States* (New York: Oxford University Press, 1982), p. 278.

32. Alice Kessler-Harris, *Out To Work,* p. 303.

33. Jacqueline Jones, *Labor of Love, Labor of Sorrow: Black Women, Work and the Family from Slavery to the Present* (New York: Basic Books, 1985), pp. 235, 258, 262.

34. Eveline M. Burns, *Social Security and Public Policy* (New York: McGraw Hill, 1956), p. 89.

35. The examples of AFDC restrictions are discussed in Linda Gordon, *Pitied but Not Entitled,* pp. 276, 414 (n. 103); Lucy Komisar, *Down and Out in the USA,* p. 83; Jacqueline Jones, *Labor of Love, Labor of Sorrow,* p. 26; Frances Fox Piven and Richard Cloward, *Regulating the Poor: The Functions of Public Welfare* (New York: Random House, 1993), pp. 128 (n. 3), 134.

36. Frances Fox Piven and Richard Cloward, *Regulating the Poor,* pp. 135, 136 (n. 17).

37. Susan M. Hartmann, *The Home Front and Beyond,* p. 165; Steven Mintz and Susan Kellog, *Domestic Revolutions,* pp. 170–72; Heather Ross and Isabel Sawhill, *Time of Transition: The Growth of Families Headed by Women* (Washington, D.C.: Urban Institute, 1975), p. 199, Table 1-M.

38. Linda Gordon, *Pitied but Not Entitled,* p. 35; Jacqueline Jones, *Labor of Love, Labor of Sorrow,* p. 263.

39. Steven Mintz and Susan Kellog, *Domestic Revolutions,* pp. 162–65; Mildred Rein, *Dilemmas of Welfare Policy: Why Work Strategies Haven't Worked* (New York: Praeger, 1982), pp. 15–16.

40. Eveline Burns, *Social Security and Public Policy,* p. 86, n. 13.

41. Daniel P. Moynihan, "Employment, Income and the Ordeal of the Negro Family," *Daedalus: Journal of the American Academy of Arts and Sciences* 94, no. 4 (Fall 1965): 762–766; Michael K. Brown, "Divergent Fates: Race, Gender and the Legacy of the New Deal," (Conference Proceedings, Institute for Women's Policy Research, Washington, D.C., 1994)

42. James Patterson, *America's Struggle Against Poverty,* pp. 89–90.

43. The examples of AFDC rules and regulations are variously discussed in Linda Gordon "What Does Welfare Regulate?" *Social Research* 55, no. 4

(Winter 1988), p. 616; Komisar, *Down and Out in the USA*, pp. 79–80, 89; Patterson, *America's Struggle Against Poverty 1900–1980*, p. 88.

44. For examples of moral behavior standards detailed in the next two paragraphs see Komisar, *Down and Out in the USA*, p. 146; Piven and Cloward, *Regulating the Poor*, pp. 139–140, 169–170; Rickie Solinger, *Wake Up Little Susie: Single Pregnancy and Race Before Roe V. Wade* (New York: Routledge, 1992), pp. 51–56.

45. U.S. Congress, House Committee on Ways and Means, *Overview of Entitlement Programs, 1994 Green Book*, pp. 89, 395.

46. Frances Fox Piven and Richard Cloward, *Regulating the Poor*. This analysis has been challenged in Walter Trattner, ed., *Social Welfare or Social Control: Some Historical Reflections on Regulating the Poor* (Knoxville, TN: University of Tennessee Press, p. 36; and James Patterson, *America's Struggle Against Poverty*, p. 134.

47. The data in this paragraph can be found in James Patterson, *America's Struggle Against Poverty*, p. 172; Heather Ross and Isabel Sawhill, *Time of Transition*, p. 105; Gilbert Y. Steiner, *The State of Welfare* (Washington, D.C.: Brookings Institution, 1971), p. 41; U.S. Congress, Joint Economic Committee, Subcommittee on Fiscal Policy, *Studies in Public Welfare*, p. 169, Table 9.

48. Quoted in James Patterson, *America's Struggle Against Poverty*, pp. 172–73; Gilbert Y. Steiner, *The State of Welfare*, p. 49; and James Patterson, Ibid., pp. 89–90.

49. Heather Ross and Isabel Sawhill, *Time of Transition*, p. 98; Mildred Rein, *Dilemmas of Welfare Policy: Why Work Strategies Haven't Worked* (New York: Praeger, 1982), pp. 8–9; Sar Levitan, Martin Rein, and David Marwick, *Work and Welfare Go Together* (Baltimore: Johns Hopkins Press, 1972), p. 14; Steiner, *The State of Welfare*, p. 41; and U.S. Congress, Joint Economic Committee, *Income Security For Americans: Recommendations of the Public Welfare Study* (Washington, D.C.: Government Printing Office, p. 72.

50. The discussion of WIN draws on Sar Levitan, Martin Rein, and David Marwick, *Work and Welfare Go Together*; Mildred Rein, *Dimensions of Welfare Policy*; Nancy Rose, *Workfare or Fair Work: Women, Welfare, and Government Work Programs* (New Brunswick, NJ: Rutgers University Press, 1995), chap. 6; U.S. Congress, Joint Economic Committee, *Income Security for Americans: Recommendations of the Public Welfare Study* (Washington, D.C.: Government Printing Office; General Accounting Office, 1974); and Comptroller General of the United States, *An Overview of the WIN Program: Its Objectives, Accomplishments and Problems* (Washington, D.C.: Government Printing Office, 1982).

51. For the data on the marital status of AFDC mothers during this period see Joel Handler and Yeheskel Hasenfeld, *The Moral Construction of Poverty*

(Newbury Park: Sage Publications, 1991), p. 114; Gilbert Y. Steiner, *The State of Welfare*, p.42; and U.S. Congress, House Committee on Ways and Means, *Overview of Entitlement Programs, 1993 Green Book*, p. 696, Table 31.

52. Johnnie Tillmon, "Welfare Is a Women's Issue," *Liberation News Service*, no. 415 (26 February 1972), reprinted in *American Working Women: A Documentary History 1600 to the Present*, Rosalyn Baxandall, Linda Gordon, and Susan Reverby (New York: Vintage Books, 1976), pp. 354–58.

53. Lucy Komisar, *Down and Out in the USA*, p. 146.

54. Rickie Solinger, Wake Up Little Susie, p. 49, citing Julius Horowitz, "The Arithmetic of Delinquency," *New York Times Magazine*, 31 January 1965, p. 12.

55. Daniel P. Moynihan, "The Negro Family: The Case For National Action," in *The Moynihan Report and the Politics of Controversy*, ed. L. Rainwater and W. Yancy (Cambridge: MIT Press, 1967), pp. 39–125.

Part 3: The Gendered Welfare State

1. The following definitions of patriarchy draw on Michelle Barrett, *Women's Oppression Today* (London: Verso, 1980); Martha Albertson Fineman, *The Neutered Mother, The Sexual Family, and Other Twentieth-Century Tragedies* (New York: Routledge, 1995); Iris Young, "Is Male Gender Identity the Cause of Male Domination?" in *Mothering Essays in Feminist Theory*, ed. Joyce Trebilcot (Totowa, NJ: Rowman and Allenheld, 1984), pp. 129–46; Gerda Lerner, *The Creation of Patriarchy* (New York: Oxford University Press, 1986); Sylvia Walby, *Patriarchy at Work* (Minneapolis: University of Minnesota Press, 1986).

2. Mimi Abramovitz, *Regulating the Lives of Women: Social Welfare Policy from Colonial Times to the Present* (Boston, MA: South End Press, 1988).

3. Evelyn Nakamo Glenn, "Racial Ethnic Women's Labor: The Intersection of Race, Gender, and Class Oppression," *Review of Radical Political Economics* 17, no. 3 (1985): 86–108.

4. See Johanna Brenner and Barbara Laslett, "Social Reproduction and the Family," in *The Social Reproduction of Organization and Culture*, ed. Ulf Himmelstrand (London: Sage Publications, 1986), pp. 115–31; Renate Bridenthal, "The Dialectics of Production and Reproduction in History," *Radical America* 10, no. 2 (March/April 1976): 3–11; Barbara Laslett, "Production, Reproduction and Social Change," in *The State of Sociology: Problems and Prospects*, ed. James F. Short, Jr. (Beverly Hills, CA: Sage, 1981), pp. 239–58; Natalie J. Sokoloff, *Between Money and Love: The Dialectics of Women's Home and Market Work* (New York: Praeger, 1981); Lise Vogel, *Marxism and the Oppression of Women: Toward a Unitary Theory* (New Brunswick, NJ: Rutgers University Press, 1983).

5. See for example, Richard Titmuss, *Essays on the Welfare State* (London: Allen and Unwin, 1958); Harold Wilensky and Charles Lebaux, *Industrial Society and Social Welfare* (New York: Russell Sage, 1958); Harold Wilensky, *The Welfare State and Equalit* (Berkeley: University of California Press, 1975).

6. T. H. Marshall, *Citizenship and Social Class* (Cambridge: Cambridge University Press, 1950); Ramish Mishra, *Society and Social Policy: Theories and Practice of Welfare* (London: Macmillan, 1981).

7. Ian Gough, *The Political Economy of Welfare* (London: Macmillan, 1979); James O'Connor, *The Fiscal Crisis of the State* (New York: St. Martin's Press, 1973); Mishra, *Society and Social Policy,* 68–96.

8. Some of the most important of these works are, in alphabetical order: Abramovitz, *Regulating the Lives of Women;* Margaret Benston, "The Political Economy of Women's Liberation," *Monthly Review* 21, no. 4 (September 1969): 13–27; Johanna Brenner and Barbara Laslett, "Gender, Social Reproduction, and Women's Self-Organization: Considering the U.S. Welfare State," *Gender and Society* 5, no. 3 (September 1991): 311–33; Brenner and Laslett, "Social Reproduction and the Family," pp. 115–31; Carol Brown, "Mothers, Fathers and Children: From Private to Public Patriarchy," in *Women and Revolution,* ed. Lydia Sargent (Boston: South End Press, 1981); Stephanie Coontz, *The Social Origins of Private Life. A History of American Families 1600–1900* (London: Verso, 1988); Maria Della Costa, *The Power of Women and the Subversion of the Community* (Bristol: Falling Wall Press, 1973), pp. 19–54; Zillah Eisenstein, *Feminism and Sexual Equality: Crisis in Liberal America* (New York: Monthly Review Press, 1984); Betty Friedan, *The Feminine Mystique* (New York: Dell, 1963); Maxine Fuller, "Sex Role Stereotyping and Social Science," in *The Sex Role System: Psychological and Sociological Perspectives,* ed. J. Chetwynd and D. Hartness (Boston: Routledge and Kegan Paul, 1978); Linda Gordon, *Pitied But Not Entitled: Single Mothers and the History of Welfare* (New York: Free Press, 1994); Linda Gordon, ed., *Women, the State and Welfare* (Madison, WI: University of Wisconsin Press, 1990); Heidi Hartmann, "The Family as the Locus of Gender, Class, and Political Struggle: The Example of Housework," *Signs* 6 (Spring 1981): 366–94; Barbara Hobson, "Economic Dependency and Women's Social Citizenship: Some Thoughts on Epsing-Anderson's Welfare State Regimes" (Paper presented at the Conference on Gender, Citizenship and Social Policy, 31 October 1991); Laslett, "Production, Reproduction and Social Change," pp. 239–58; Mary McIntosh, *The State and the Oppression of Women,* in *Feminism and Materialism,* ed. Annette Kuhn and Anne Wolpe (London: Routledge and Kegan Paul, 1978), pp. 254–89; Steven Mintz and Susan Kellog, *Domestic Revolutions: A Social History of American Family Life* (New York: Free Press, 1988); Robyn

Muncy, *Creating a Female Dominion in American Reform, 1890–1935* (New York: Oxford University Press, chaps. 2 and 3; Mary O'Brien, *The Politics of Reproduction* (London: Routledge and Kegan Paul, 1981); Ann S. Orloff, "Gender and the Social Rights of Citizenship: The Comparative Analysis of Gender Relations and Welfare States," *American Sociological Review* 58, no. 3 (June 1993): 303–28; Theda Skocpol, *Protecting Soldiers and Mothers: The Political Origins of Social Policy in the United States* (Cambridge, MA: Harvard University Press, 1992); Karen Skold, "The Interests of Feminists and Children in Child Care" in *Feminism, Children, and the New Families,* ed. S.M. Dornbusch & M.H. Strober (New York: Guilford Press, 1988), pp. 113–36; Sokoloff, *Between Money and Love;* Barbara Thorne, "Feminist Rethinking of the Family: An Overview," in *Rethinking the Family: Some Feminist Questions,* ed. Barbara Thorne and Marilyn Yalom (New York: Longman, 1982), pp. 1–24; Vogel, *Marxism and the Oppression of Women;* Susan Ware, *Beyond Suffrage: Women in the New Deal* (Cambridge, MA: Harvard University Press, 1981); Batya Weinbaum and Amy Bridges, "The Other Side of the Paycheck: Monopoly Capital and the Structure of Consumption," *Monthly Review* 28 (July/August 1976): 88–103; Elizabeth Wilson, *Women and the Welfare State* (London: Tavistock, 1977); Maxine Baca Zinn, "Family, Feminism and Race in America," *Gender & Society* 4, no. 1 (March 1990): 68–82; Eli Zaretsky, "The Place of the Family in the Origins of the Welfare State," in *Rethinking the Family,* ed. Thorne and Yalom, pp. 1–24.

9. Abramovitz, *Regulating the Lives of Women;* McIntosh, "The State and the Oppression of Women," pp. 254–89; O'Brien, *The Politics of Reproduction;* Wilson, *Women and the Welfare State;* Virginia Sapiro, "The Gender Basis of American Social Policy," in *Women, the State, and Welfare,* ed. Gordon, pp. 36–55.

10. Hobson, "Economic Dependency and Women's Social Citizenship"; Hartmann, "The Family as the Locus of Gender, Class, and Political Struggle," pp. 366–94; Coontz, *The Social Origins of Private Life;* Susan Schecter, *Women and Male Violence* (Boston, MA: South End Press, 1982); Linda Gordon, "Family Violence, Feminism, and Social Control," in Gordon, *Women, the State and Welfare,* pp. 178–99; Orloff, "Gender and the Social Rights of Citizenship," pp. 303–28.

11. Patricia Ann Collins, *Black Feminist Thought: Knowledge, Consciousness and the Politics of Empowerment* (New York: Harper Collins, 1990), pp. 43–66; Glenn, "Racial Ethnic Women's Labor," pp. 86–108; Zinn, "Family, Feminism and Race in America," pp. 68–82.

12. Linda Gordon, "The New Feminist Scholarship on the Welfare State," in *Women, the State, and Welfare,* ed. Gordon, pp 35; Barbara Nelson, "The Origins of the Two-Channel Welfare State: Workmen's Compensation and

Mother's Aid," in *Women, the State and Welfare*, ed. Gordon, pp. 123–51; Sapiro, "The Gender Basis of American Social Policy," pp. 36–55.

13. See, for example, Nancy Fraser and Linda Gordon, "Contract Versus Charity: Why There Is No Social Citizenship in the United States," *Socialist Review* 22, no. 3 (July/August 1992): 45–67; Orloff, "Gender and the Social Rights of Citizenship," pp. 303–28; Orloff, "Gender and the Welfare State," *American Review of Sociology* 22 (1996); Carole Pateman, "The Patriarchal Welfare State," in *Democracy and the Welfare State*, ed. Amy Gutmann (Princeton, NJ: Princeton University Press, 1988), pp. 231–60.

14. For a discussion of this, see Zillah Eisenstein, "Constructing a Theory of Capitalist Patriarchy and Socialist Feminism," in *Women, Class and the Feminist Imagination*, ed. K. Hansen and I. Philipson (Philadelphia, PA: Temple University Press, 1990), pp. 114–45; Vogel, *Marxism and the Oppression of Women*.

15. Gough, *The Political Economy of Welfare;* O'Connor, *The Fiscal Crisis of the State*.

16. Gordon, *Pitied But Not Entitled;* Gwendolyn Mink, *The Wages of Motherhood: Inequality in the Welfare State, 1917–1942* (Ithaca, NY: Cornell University Press, 1995), p. 1.

17. Hartmann, "The Unhappy Marriage of Marxism and Feminism," pp. 1–43; Eisenstein, *Feminism and Sexual Equality,* Sokoloff, *Between Money and Love;* Walby, *Patriarchy at Work;* McIntosh, "The State and the Oppression of Women," pp. 253–89; Pateman, "The Patriarchal Welfare State," pp. 231–60; Frances Fox Piven, "Women, the State and Ideology," in *Gender and the Life Course*, ed. Alice Rossi (New York: Aldine, 1985).

18. See Abramovitz, *Regulating the Lives of Women*, pp. 254–60; Jane Ross and Melinda Opp, "Treatment of Women In the U.S. Social Security System," *Social Security Bulletin* 53, no. 3 (1993): 56–67; Maxine Ferber, "Women's Employment and the Social Security System," *Social Security Bulletin* 56, no. 3 (1993): 43–55.

19. Brenner and Laslett, "Social Reproduction and the Family," pp. 120–21; Bridenthal, "The Dialectics of Production and Reproduction in History," pp. 3–11; Carol Ehrlich, "The Unhappy Marriage of Marxism and Feminism: Can It Be Saved?" in *Women and Revolution: A Discussion of the Unhappy Marriage of Marxism and Feminism*, ed. Lydia Sargent (Boston, MA: South End Press, 1981), pp. 109–35; McIntosh, "The State and the Oppression of Women," pp. 254–89; O'Brien, *The Politics of Reproduction;* Sokoloff, *Between Money and Love;* Young, "Beyond the Unhappy Marriage: A Critique of the Dual Systems Theory," pp. 43–71.

20. Zillah Eisenstein, *The Radical Future of Liberal Feminism* (New York: Longman, 1981).

21. Orloff, "Gender and the Social Rights of Citizenship," pp. 303–28; Nancy

Fraser, "After the Family Wage: What Do Women Want In Social Welfare," in "Women and Welfare Reform: A Policy Conference" (Proceedings of conference sponsored by the Institute For Women's Policy Research, Washington, D.C., 23 October 1993).

22. Pateman, "The Patriarchal Welfare State," pp. 231–60.

Part 4: Fighting Back: From the Legislature to the Academy to the Streets

1. Guida West and Rhoda Lois Blumberg, *Women and Social Protest* (New York: Oxford University Press, 1990), p. 7.

2. See Walter Korpi, *The Working Class and Welfare Capitalism: Work, Unions and Politics in Sweden* (London: Routledge & Kegan Paul, 1978), chap. 1; Ramesh Mishra, *Society and Social Policy: Theories and Practice of Welfare*, 2nd ed. (London: Macmillan, 1981), chaps. 1 and 2.

3. Gosta Epsing-Anderson, *Three Worlds of Welfare Capitalism* (Princeton, NJ: Princeton University Press, 1990); Gosta Epsing-Anderson, *Politics Against Markets: The Social Democratic Road to Power* (Princeton, NJ: Princeton University Press, 1985); Korpi, *The Working Class and Welfare Capitalism*.

4. Korpi, *The Working Class and Welfare Capitalism*, pp. 5–10; Mishra, *Society and Social Policy*, pp. 68–87; Paul M. Sweezy, *The Theory of Capitalist Development* (New York: Monthly Review Press, 1968), pp. 244–50.

5. Diane Balser, *Sisterhood and Solidarity: Feminism and Labor in Modern Times* (Boston, MA: South End Press, 1987); Philip Foner, *Women and the American Labor Movement from World War I to the Present* (New York: Free Press, 1980); Barbara Kingsolver, *Women in the Great Arizona Mine Strike of 1983* (Ithaca, NY: ILR Press, 1989); Ruth Milkman, ed., *Women, Work, and Protest: A Century of U.S. Women's Labor History* (Boston, MA: Routledge & Kegan Paul, 1985).

6. Ann Bookman and Sandra Morgen, eds., *Women and the Politics of Empowerment* (Philadelphia, PA: Temple University Press, 1988); Nancy Hewitt and Suzanne Lebsock, *Visible Women: New Essays on American Activism* (Urbana, IL: University of Illinois Press, 1991); Ida Susser, *Norman Street: Poverty and Politics In an Urban Neighborhood* (New York: Oxford University Press, 1982); Ann Gibson Robinson, *The Montgomery Bus Boycott and the Women Who Started It* (Knoxville: University of Tennessee Press, 1987); Nancy Naples, "Contradictions in the Gender Subtext of the War on Poverty: The Community Work and Resistance of Women from Low-Income Communities," *Social Problems* 38, no. 3 (1991): 316–32.

7. Linda Gordon, *Heroes of Their Own Lives: The Politics and History of Family Violence* (New York: Penguin Books, 1988); Susan Handley Hertz, *The Welfare Mothers Movement: A Decade of Change for Poor Women*

NOTES

(Washington, D.C.: University Press of America, 1981); Megan H. Morrissey, "The Downtown Welfare Advocate Center: A Case Study of a Welfare Rights Organization," *Social Service Review* 64, no. 2 (June 1990): 189–20; Frances Fox Piven and Richard A. Cloward, *Poor People's Movements: Why They Succeed, How They Fail* (New York: Vintage Books, 1979), pp. 264–362; Jackie Pope, "Women in the Welfare Rights Struggle: The Brooklyn Welfare Action Council," in *Women and Social Protest,* ed. West and Blumberg, pp. 57–74; Guida West, *The National Welfare Rights Movement: The Social Protest of Poor Women* (New York: Praeger, 1981).

8. Kathleen Blee, "Family Patterns and the Politicization of Consumption Relations," *Sociological Spectrum* 5, no. 4 (1985): 295–316; Dana Frank, "Housewives, Socialists, and the Politics of Food: The 1917 Cost-of-Living Protests," *Feminist Studies* 11, no. 2 (1985): 265–85; Paula Hyman, Immigrant Women and Consumer Protest: The New York City Kosher "Meat Boycott of 1902," *American Jewish History* 70 (Summer 1980): 91–105; Tamar Kaplan, "Female Consciousness and Collective Action: Barcelona, 1910–1918," *Signs* 7 (1982): 545–65; Barbara Laslett and Johanna Brenner, "Gender and Social Reproduction: Historical Perspectives," *Annual Review of Sociology* 15 (1989):381–404; Batya Weinbaum and Amy Bridges, "The Other Side of the Paycheck: Monopoly Capital and the Structure of Consumption," in *Capitalist Patriarchy and the Case For Socialist Feminism,* ed. Zillah Eisenstein (New York: Monthly Review Press, 1979), pp. 90–205.

9. George Rudé, *The Crowd in History* (New York: Wiley, 1964).

10. The discussion of nineteenth-century reform draws on: Eleanor Flexner, *Century of Struggle: The Women' s Rights Movement in the United States* (New York: Atheneum, 1968); Nancy E. McGlen and Karen O'Conner, *Women's Rights: The Struggle for Equality in the Nineteenth and Twentieth Centuries* (New York: Praeger, 1983); Mary Ryan, *Womanhood in America. From Colonial Times to the Present* (New York: New Viewpoints, 1975), pp. 137–92; Theda Skocpol, *Protecting Soldiers and Mothers: The Political Origins of Social Policy in the United States* (Cambridge, MA: Harvard University Press, 1992).

11. The discussion of Progressive Era and New Deal activism by white women draws on: Johanna Brenner and Barbara Laslett, "Gender, Social Reproduction, and Women's Self-Organization: Considering the U.S. Welfare State," *Gender and Society* 5, no. 3 (September 1991): 311–33; Linda Gordon, *Pitied But Not Entitled: Single Mothers and the History of Welfare* (New York: Free Press, 1994); Robyn Muncy, *Creating a Female Dominion in American Reform, 1890–1935* (New York: Oxford University Press, 1991), chaps. 2 and 3; Skocpol, *Protecting Soldiers and Mothers;* Susan Ware, *Beyond Suffrage: Women in the New Deal* (Cambridge, MA: Harvard University Press, 1981).

12. The phenomenon of female social reform was not unique to the United States. During the same period, intense activism by European women helped to forge the modern welfare state in France and Britain. See Beth Koven and Sonya Michel, "Womanly Duties: Maternalist Politics and the Origins of Welfare States in France, Germany, Great Britain, and the United States" (unpub. ms., 19 October 1990).

13. The debate about whether social policy that treats women as equals of men is better for women than social policy that treats women and men differently based on their unique differences has continued to rage.

14. The discussion of Progressive Era and New Deal activism among African-American women draws on: Eileen Boris, "The Power of Motherhood: Black and White Activist Women Redefine the Political," in *Mothers of a New World: Maternalist Politics and the Origins of the Welfare State,* ed. Beth Koven and Sonya Michel (New York: Routledge, 1993), pp. 213–46; Angela Davis, *Women, Race, and Class* (New York: Vintage, 1983); Paula Giddings, *When and Where I Enter: The Impact of Black Women on Race and Sex in America* (Toronto: Bantam Books, 1984); Gordon, *Pitied But Not Entitled,* chap. 5; Darlene Clark Hine, "Lifting the Veil, Shattering the Silence: Black Women's History in Slavery and Freedom," in *The State of Afro-American History, Past, Present and Future,* ed. D. C. Hine (Baton Rouge: Louisiana State University Press, 1986), pp. 223–52; Gerda Lerner, *Black Women in White America: A Documentary History* (New York: Vintage Books, 1973); Gwendolyn Mink, *The Wages of Motherhood: Inequality in the Welfare State, 1917–1942* (Ithaca, NY: Cornell University Press, 1995); Ann Firor Scott, "On Seeing and Not Seeing: A Case of Historical Invisibility," *Journal of American History* 7 (June 1984): 7–21; Deborah Gray White, "The Cost of Club Work, the Price of Black Feminism," in *Visible Women: New Essays On American Activism* (Urbana: University of Illinois Press, 1993), pp. 247–69.

15. Laslett and Brenner, "Gender and Social Reproduction," pp. 381–404

16. Gordon, *Pitied But Not Entitled;* Alice Kessler Harris, "Women and Welfare: Public Interventions in Private Lives," *Radical History Review* 56 (1993): 127–36.

17. Dorothy Gallagher, review of *Florence Kelly and the Nation's Work* by Kathryn Kish Sklar, *New York Times Book Review,* 9 July 1995, p. 9.

18. Gordon, *Pitied But Not Entitled,* pp. 55–56; Koven and Michel, "Womanly Duties"; Aileen Kraditor, *Ideas of the Women's Suffrage Movement, 1880–1920* (New York: W. W. Norton, 1981), p. 67; Muncy, *Creating a Female Dominion in American Reform.*

19. Dana Frank, "Food Wins All Struggles: Seattle Labor and the Politicization of Consumption," *Radical History Review* 51 (1991): 65–89.

20. For a detailed discussion of these events, see Frank, "Housewives, Socialists,

and the Politics of Food," *Feminist Studies* (1995) pp. 265–85; William Frieburger, "War, Prosperity, and Hunger: The New York Food Riots," *Labor History* 25 (Spring 1984): 217–39; Hyman, "Immigrant Women and Consumer Protest," pp. 91–105; Annelise Orleck, "Common Sense and a Little Fire: Working-Class Women's Activism in the Twentieth Century United States" (Ph.D. diss., New York University, 1989), pp. 540–42; Judith Smith, "Our Own Kind: Family and Networks in Providence," in *A Heritage of Her Own: Toward a New Social History of American Women*, ed. Nancy Cott and Elizabeth H. Pleck (New York: Simon and Schuster, 1979), pp. 393–411.

21. Lerner, *Black Women in White America*, pp. 211–12.

22. John Ehrenreich, *The Altruistic Imagination: A History of Social Work and Social Policy in the United States* (Ithaca, NY: Cornell University Press, 1985), p. 49; William Graebner, *The Engineering of Consent: Democracy and Authority in Twentieth-Century America* (Madison, WI: University of Wisconsin Press, 1987), pp. 58–59.

23. Ruth Schwartz Cowan, "Two Washes in the Morning and a Bridge Party at Night: The American Housewife Between the Wars," *Women's Studies* 3 (1976): 147–72; Heidi Hartmann, *Capitalism and Women's Work in the Home, 1900–1950* (Ph.D. diss., Yale University, 1984), pp. 68–69.

24. Orleck, *Common Sense and a Little Fire*, pp. 556–50.

25. Unless otherwise noted, the discussion of the community-based cost of living protests during the 1920s, 1930s, and 1940s draws on Orleck, *Common Sense and a Little Fire*, chap. 8, "We Are That Mythic Thing Called the Public Militant Housewives During the Great Depression," pp. 534–609.

26. Anne Stein, "Postwar Consumer Boycotts," *Radical America* 9 (July–August 1975): 156–61.

27. The discussion these groups is based largely on Verta Taylor, "Social Movement Continuity: The Women's Movement in Abeyance," *American Sociological Review* 54, no. 5 (October 1989): 761–76; Leila Rupp and Verta Taylor, *Survival in the Doldrums: The American Women's Rights Movement, 1945 to the 1960s* (New York: Oxford University Press, 1987).

28. Jo Ann Gibson Robinson, *The Montgomery Bus Boycott and the Women Who Started It* (Knoxville: University of Tennessee Press, 1987); Janelle Scott, "Local Leadership in the Woman Suffrage Movement: Houston's Campaign for the Vote, 1917–1918," *Houston Review* 12, no. 1 (1990): 3–22.

29. For example, the NAACP leadership included Ruby Hurley (youth director), Daisy Bates (president, Little Rock, Arkansas, chapter), Rosa Parks (secretary, Montgomery, Alabama, chapter), and Ella Baker (president, New York City chapter and national director of branch work). Women were also active in the Urban League (formed in 1911); the Congress of Racial Equality

(1943); the National Negro Labor Council (1951); the Southern Christian Leadership Conference (1957); and the Student Non-Violent Coordinating Committee (1960).

30. Giddings, *When and Where I Enter,* pp. 291–92.

31. Shulamit Reinharz, "Women as Competent Community Builders: The Other Side of the Coin," in *Social and Psychological Problems of Women: Prevention and Crisis,* ed. Annette U. Rickel, Meg Gerrard and Ira Iscoe (Washington, D.C.: Hemisphere Publishing Corporation, 1984), pp. 19–43; Jacqueline Jones, *Labor of Love, Labor of Sorrow: Black Women, Work, and the Family from Slavery to the Present* (New York: Basic Books, 1985), pp. 310–21.

32. Susan Lynn, *Progressive Women in Conservative Times: Racial Justice, Peace, and Feminism, 1945–1960* (New Brunswick, NJ: Rutgers University Press, 1992); Mrya Marx Ferree and Beth B. Hess, *Controversy and Coalition: The New Feminist Movement* (Boston, MA: Twayne Publishers, 1985).

33. William Henry Chafe, *The American Woman: Her Changing Social, Economic and Political Roles, 1920–1970* (London: Oxford University Press, 1974); Sara Evans, *Born for Liberty: A History of Women in America* (New York: Free Press, 1989).

34. The discussion of welfare rights before the formation of the National Welfare Rights Organization relies on Hertz, *The Welfare Mothers' Movement;* Morrissey, "The Downtown Welfare Advocate Center," pp. 189–207; Piven and Cloward, *Poor People's Movements,* pp. 264–362; Pope, "Women in the Welfare Rights Struggle," pp. 57–74.

35. Unless otherwise noted, this discussion of the National Welfare Rights Organization relies on Martha Davis, "Welfare Rights and Women's Rights in the 1960s" (Paper presented at the Integrating the Sixties Conference, Washington, D.C., 30 May 1995); Piven and Cloward, *Poor People's Movements,* pp. 264–362; West, *The National Welfare Rights Movement.*

36. The percent of white women on welfare rose from 46.9 percent in 1973 to 50.2 percent in 1977, while the percent of black women on welfare fell off. See West, *The National Welfare Rights Movement,* p. 262.

37. Johnnie Tillmon, "Welfare is a Women's Issue," in Rosalyn Baxandall, Linda Gordon, and Susan L Reverby, eds., *American Working Women: A Documentary History 1600 to the Present* (New York: Vintage Books, 1976), p. 358.

38. Martha Davis, "Welfare Rights and Women's Rights in the 1960s," pp. 21–22.

39. "Break Down The Wall of Poverty," *Survival News,* vol. 3, no. 2 (Summer/Fall 1989), p. 1; "Welfare Rights Turns Up The Heat, Takes Over Michigan Office," *People's Tribune,* February 5, 1990, p. 3; "No Heat, No Peace Michigan Struggle Grows, Support The Inkster 9!" *People's Tribune,*

March 5, 1990, p. 3; "Up and Out of Poverty Campaign Tours Los Angeles," *Survival News,* vol. 3, no. 2 (Summer/Fall 1989),p. 1.

40. *Welfare Mother's Voice,* Winter 1990, p. 16; "Up and Out of Poverty Campaign Goes To Wisconsin," *Survival News,* vol. 3, no. 1 (Spring 1989), p. 20.

41. Testimony of Marian Kramer, President, National Welfare Rights Union, before the Subcommittee on Human Resources, Government Operations Committee, Washington, D.C., March 10, 1994, p. 1.

42. Mary Jo Hetzel and Jackie Dee King, "Attacks on welfare heat up on national level," *Survival News,* Spring 1994, p. 9.

43. Testimony of Marian Kramer, President, National Welfare Rights Union, before the Subcommittee on Human Resources, Government Operations Committee, Washington, D.C., March 10, 1994, p. 2.

44. Update and Recent Activities of Grassroots Groups," *Linking the Neighborhods,* Welfare Law Center, May 1997, p. 4; Annie Boone, "Mother's Day Was JAMMIn", *JEDI News,* vol. 5, no. 5 (June 1997), p. 1.

45. Nancy Hobbs, "JEDI for Women Forces Policy Makers To Pay Attention," *Salt Lake Tribune,* February 26, 1998, p. C1, reprinted in *Linking Neighborhoods,* Welfare Law Center, May 1998, p. 42.

46. Photo in *Survival News,* vol. 9, no. 1 (Summer/Fall 1995), p. 1.

47. Schuyler, Nina, "Under Attack But Fighting Back. The Birth of the Poor Women's Movement," *On the Issues,* Winter 1992, pp. 22–28.

48. *Survival News,* vol. 8, no. 2 (Fall/Winter 1994), p. 29.

49. Welfare Law Center, Directory of Low Income Organizations Working on Welfare Issues, 4th ed (New York: April 1999).

50. "Update and Recent Activities of Grassroots Groups," *Linking the Neighborhoods,* Welfare Law Center, May 1997, p. 4.

51. Martha Davis, *Brutal Need,: Lawyers and the Welfare Rights Movement, 1960–1973* (New Haven: Yale University Press, 1993).

52. "Supreme Court Rejects Two Tier Welfare Benefits," *Clasp Update,* June 19, 1999, pp. 6–7; "Welfare Litigation Developments Since the PRA: An Overview," *Welfare News,* vol. 2, no. 5 (November 1997), pp. 5–6; "Organizing and Litigation: Joint Strategies for Secure Protestion for Workfare Workers," *Welfare News,* vol. 3, no. 5 (November 1998), p. 1.

53. Richard Marlim, "Legislation: A Means or an End?" *Survival News,* vol. 12, no. 2 (Spring 1998), p. 8.

54. Article 23 of the Declaration of Human Rights says that everyone has the right to work, free choice of employment, to just pay and to join unions. Article 25 declares that everyone has the right to a standard of living adequate for the health and well–being of themselves and their families and that mothers and children are entitled to special care and assistance whether born in or out of wedlock. Article 26 speaks to the rights of all to education.

The United States has signed but not ratified the treaty containing these articles.

55. KWRU leaflet inviting people to "Join the October 1999 March of the Americas." "Update and Recent Activities of Grassroots Groups," *Linking the Neighborhoods*, Welfare Law Center (New York: May 1997), p. 4; KWRU leaflets, reprinted in *Linking the Neighborhoods*, Welfare Law Center (New York: May 1998), p. 40.

56. "Acorn Wins Wage Increases; organizes workfare recipients," *Survival News*, vol. 12, no. 2 (Winter 1998), p. 17.

57. "Low Income Groups From 12 States Gather at Western Region Welfare Activists Summit," *Linking the Neighborhoods*, Welfare Law Center (New York: September 1998), pp. 2–3; Upcoming Events," *Linking the Neighborhoods*, Welfare Law Center (New York: July 1998), p. 3.

58. Diane Dujon, "Poor People's Summit Reaches Across Borders," *Survival News*, Fall 1998 (Special Section, NP) ; Healther Gonzales, "Activists Rally for Welfare/ Workfare Justice," *Survival News*, vol. 12, no. 1 (Winter 1998), pp. 1, 4; Dottie Stevens, "Which Way Welfare Rights?" *Survival News*, Spring/Summer 1999, p. 5.

59. Liu Caitlin, "Activists Call for End to Welfare Limits," *Los Angeles Times*, August 19, 1999.

60. Ann Withorn, *Not For Lack of Trying: The Struggle Over Welfare Reform in Massachusetts 1992–1998* (Boston: John W. McCormack Institute For Public Affairs, March 1999), pp. 10–12; Ann Withorn, "Workers' Rights and Welfare Rights: What's The Connection?" *Survival News*, vol. 12, no. 2 (Spring 1998), p. 5.

61. "National Welfare Monitoring and Advocacy Project Promotes Monitory in Advocacy and Organizing CWLC Joins as Partner," *Linking the Neighborhoods*, Welfare Law Center (New York: December 1998), p. 5–6.

62. *Women and Welfare Watch*, NOW Legal Defense and Educational Fund, Spring 1999, p. 1.

63. Barbara Bergman & Heidi Hartmann, "A Welfare Reform Based on Help for Working Parents," *Feminist Economics*, vol. 1, no. 2 (1995), pp. 85–89.

64. Nancy Fraser, "After The Family Wage: What Do Women Want In Social Welfare," in *Women and Welfare Reform: A Policy Conference* (Washington D.C.: October 23, 1993), co–sponsored by the Institute For Women's Policy Research.

65. Ann S. Orloff, "Gender and the Social Rights of Citizenship: The Comparative Analysis of Gender Relations and Welfare States," *American Sociological Review*, vol. 58, no. 3 (June 1993), pp. 303–328.

66. Martha Albertson Fineman, *The Neutered Mother, The Sexual Family, and Other Twentieth Century Tragedies* (New York: Routledge, 1995).

INDEX

abortion, 37, 39, 48, 157–58*n*
abstinence programs, 37–38
ACORN (Association of Community
    Organizations for Reform Now),
    144, 145
activism: by middle-class women,
    117–22; post- TANF, 142–52;
    post-World War II, 128–31; wel-
    fare rights organizing, 131–42;
    by working-class women, 122–27
Advocacy for Resources for Modern
    Survival (ARMS), 138
AFDC UP program, 80, 82
African-Americans, *see* **Blacks**
Aid to the Blind (AB), 16, 65
Aid to Dependent Children (ADC), 16,
    63–66; becomes Aid to Families
    with Dependent Children, 76;
    post-World War II attacks on,
    67–71, 73–75
Aid to Families with Dependent Chil-
    dren (AFDC), 16; during 1960s
    and 1970s, 81–83; Aid to Depen-
    dent Children becomes, 76;
    attacks upon, 19–21, 77–78; con-
    verted into block grants, 142;

cuts in, 23–25; extensions to,
    76–77; marriage discouraged by,
    40; Mothers' Pensions, forerun-
    ner of, 61–63; pregnant women
    under, 107; welfare rights orga-
    nizing and, 132
Aid to the Permanently and Totally
    Disabled (APTD), 16
Alabama, 74
Alameda County (California) Welfare
    Rights Organization, 132
almshouses, 55
American Enterprise Institute, 19
American Women Suffrage Associa-
    tion, 117
Arizona, 79
Arkansas, 39, 71, 72, 74
Association of Community Organiza-
    tions for Reform Now
    (ACORN), 144, 145

Baker, Ella, 170*n*
banks, 31
Bates, Daisy, 170*n*
battering (domestic violence), 48
Bethune, Mary McLeod, 120